Fractional Ownership & REITS

Real Estate Investment Avenues

Dr. Adv. HARSHUL SAVLA

Ph.D (MU), MMS (JBIMS), LL.M (MU), LL.B (GLC), BMS (NM)

INDIA • SINGAPORE • MALAYSIA

Notion Press

No.8, 3rd Cross Street,
CIT Colony, Mylapore,
Chennai, Tamil Nadu – 600004

First Published by Notion Press 2021
Copyright © Dr. Adv. Harshul Savla 2021
All Rights Reserved.

ISBN 978-1-63850-589-1

This book has been published with all efforts taken to make the material error-free after the consent of the author. However, the author and the publisher do not assume and hereby disclaim any liability to any party for any loss, damage, or disruption caused by errors or omissions, whether such errors or omissions result from negligence, accident, or any other cause.

While every effort has been made to avoid any mistake or omission, this publication is being sold on the condition and understanding that neither the author nor the publishers or printers would be liable in any manner to any person by reason of any mistake or omission in this publication or for any action taken or omitted to be taken or advice rendered or accepted on the basis of this work. For any defect in printing or binding the publishers will be liable only to replace the defective copy by another copy of this work then available.

TESTIMONIALS

"I have known Dr. Harshul as a through Real Estate Professional who is very well versed about the Sector, I'm sure his experiences will help one and all"

SBI's First Woman Chairperson, Arundhati Bhattacharya

"Congratulations! Dr Harshul for your amazing endeavor of creating one of India's most comprehensive literature on the Real Estate Sector. It is an excellent series of books and great learning for those who have it. I know that you will soon have a much larger audience for your work"

National President NAREDCO, Dr. Niranjan Hiranandani

"This is one of the most comprehensive set of Real Estate Literature, I strongly recommend to all"

President Elect CREDAI National, Boman Irani (Rustomjee)

"Adv. Harshul Savla is a budding and promising Entrepreneur in Real Estate Industry in MMR region with keen insight and grasp of Strategy, Numbers and Statistics. He is a great addition to the Managing Committee Team of CREDAI MCHI"

President CREDAI MCHI, Deepak Goradia (Dosti Realty)

Testimonials

"Harshul is known to me for a decade, he is an astute Advocate and a celebrated Author. His understanding of Real Estate and its nuances is exhaustive. His work will be a reference guide / point for the new entrants in the sector"

President NAREDCO Maharashtra, Ashok Mohanani (Ekta World)

"Real Estate is a very vast subject. There are very few who understand the theoretical and practical nuances of Real Estate Sector, I am glad to note that you have studied the same in great depth and your analysis will be very helpful to the industry."

Chief Engineer (Development Plan) MCGM, Shri V.P. Chithore

"Adv. Harshul Savla has a very good exposure and knowledge of the Real Estate Sector. He has excellent vocabulary skills and speaks with confidence and clarity on matters of Real Estate. I feel his commitment of sharing knowledge inspires many young Real Estate professionals and he is truly focused on bringing a positive impact in the industry in times to come"

President PEATA India, Ar. Samir Hingoo

"Harshul was part of my team, assisting me in executing my responsibilities as a core team member of JLL India. He has a deep understanding of the Real Estate market, trends and policies"

Former CEO & Country Head – JLL India, Ramesh Nair

"Well Researched, I wish this Book all the Success!"

President Bombay Management Association & Director JBIMS, Dr. Kavita Laghate

"Harshul Savla presents a perfect blend of academia and practical hands-on experience. I am proud to see him excel in all fields"

Former Director JBIMS, Dr. Chandrahauns Chavan

"Dr. Harshul is an avid researcher on the subject of Real Estate. I am sure readers will find his work of immense value to them"

Head Department of Law - University of Mumbai, Dr. Rajeshri Varhadi

"Advocate Harshul is a thoughtful researcher and a prolific writer, his ability to make most complex subject; simple and lucid is remarkable. He is extremely insightful on the subject matter of Real Estate. I'm sure he will produce a good read"

CEO Haj Committee of India & Former Registrar University of Mumbai, Dr. M.A. Khan

"I have mentored Harshul's Ph.D. thesis and I am extremely proud of his Research Skills"

Head of Research Department, Sydenham Institute of Management Studies, Dr. R.K. Srivastava

"This book is a must read for all; I personally endorse Dr. Harshul's Research"

CEO Wockhardt Foundation & Executive Director Wockhardt Ltd., Sir Dr. Huzaifa Khorakiwala

"I am sure Dr. Harshul's books will be an ideal start for anyone wanting to understand about Real Estate Sector in India"

COO - P.D. Hinduja Hospital & Medical Research Centre, Joy Chakraborty

"Harshul has a perfect understanding of issues being faced by the Built Environment. He is an excellent Research person, a good mentor for young talent and we are proud to have him on our panel of Guest Faculty at RICS SBE"

Associate Dean & Director – RICS School Built Environment, Amity University Mumbai, Amol Shimpi

"Harshul is one of the young and upcoming participants of today's real estate industry and I'm sure he will go on to shape and influence it in future"

Director Kanakia Group, Ashish Kanakia

"I wish Dr. Harshul's initiative on contributing content around Real Estate in India via this book all the success!"

Director – Asia Pacific Capital Markets, JLL, Priyank Shah

ABOUT THE AUTHOR

Dr. Adv. Harshul Savla (MRICS)

Dr. Adv. Harshul Savla (MRICS) is a Principal Partner of M Realty (Suvidha Lifespaces) which has successfully completed more than 1.2 million sq. ft. in the last 30 years across Mumbai City under the able leadership of Mr. Pramesh Rambhiya. CRISIL India recognized Dr. Harshul as "Young Thought Leader", and Realty NXT featured him as "Young Turk of Real Estate Sector". He has won the prestigious CREDAI-MCHI Golden Pillar Award in the category of Best Debutant Real Estate Developer and has been awarded "Young Achiever of the Year" by ET NOW, CNN News 18, ZEE Business, MAHARASHTRA Times, ABP News, MID DAY and Realty Quarter.

Dr. Harshul has worked as EA to Ramesh Nair, CEO and Country Head at JLL, India and has worked in the Wealth Management Team at TATA Capital. He is a perfect blend of Corporate Experience along with stellar education credentials of Ph.D, LL.M, LL.B, MBA and

BMS. Apart from this, he is an NSE Certified Market Professional - Level 4 and has done a course on 'Strategic Real Estate Management' from ISB, Hyderabad. As a matter of fact, he is one of the youngest Office Bearer in the Managing Committee of CREDAI-MCHI, wherein he is the Convener of Research & Analytics Wing and looks into the Learning and Development Initiatives.

Dr. Harshul is also an Amazon Best Selling Author and has authored one of India's most comprehensive books on the Real Estate Sector. Some of his books are ERA Post-RERA, Real Estate Laws, Reality of Realty, Real Estate Valuation, Affordable Housing, NBFC & HFC Crisis, Fractional Ownership & REITs, Insolvency & Bankruptcy Code, Self-Redevelopment & Reviving Stalled Projects, Luxury Retail and COVID-O-NOMICS. He regularly writes articles for the fortnightly business magazine Property House.

Dr. Harshul is also a Visiting Faculty at the prestigious RICS School of Built Environment, Mumbai Campus. Harshul teaches the subject 'Real Estate Development Process' to Management Students at the Mumbai Campus. He is also Guest Lecturer at REMI - The Real Estate Management Institute, Mumbai. He was Invited to conduct Session on REITs in India for Developers Members of NAREDCO and was one of the youngest Member Developer to do so. He has also delivered a lecture at PEATA (I) on the Future of Realty.

RESEARCH TEAM

Bhavesh Patil

PGDM – Real Estate Management (SBM NMIMS), B.E. - Civil Engineering

Research Intern, M Realty

Varun CH

PGDM - Real Estate Management (SBM NMIMS)

Research Intern, M Realty

Vishal Jain

MBA – Real Estate and Urban Infrastructure (RICS SBE)

Editor & Management Trainee, M Realty

CONTENTS

1. WHY INVEST IN REAL ESTATE?

1.1 Reasons to Invest in Real Estate	15
1.2 Why Real estate in Covid'19 Crisis?	17
1.3 Consumer Sentiment Surveys	17
1.4 Real Estate vs Other options	18
1.5 Comparison Factors	21
1.6 Summary	25

2. REAL ESTATE AS AN ASSET CLASS

2.1 What is an Asset Class?	27
2.2 Residential asset class	27
2.3 Commercial asset class	32
2.4 Retail asset class	36
2.5 Industrial asset class	40

3. HOW TO INVEST IN REAL ESTATE

3.1 Primary vs Secondary Market	43
3.2 Ways to Invest in Real Estate by buying property	44
3.3 Ways to Invest in Real Estate Without Buying Property	52

4. SOURCES OF INCOME IN REAL ESTATE

4.1	Income from physical investments	57
4.2	Income from non-physical investments	61

5. REAL ESTATE INVESTMENT TRUSTS (REITs)

5.1	Overview	63
5.2	Structure of a REIT	64
5.3	How does a REIT work?	66
5.4	Types of REITs	66
5.5	How to Invest?	68
5.6	Advantages of Investing in REITs	68

6. GLOBAL REITs

6.1	Introduction	70
6.2	REIT Index and Organizations	71
6.3	Stages of REITs Globally	72
6.4	Structures of REIT	74
6.5	Comparison	79
6.6	Correlations across borders	83
6.7	Investment in International REITs	83

7. REITs IN INDIA

7.1	Introduction	85
7.2	REIT-able cities in India	86
7.3	REIT Regulations	88
7.4	REIT Tax Implications	89

8. CASE STUDY ON REITs

8.1	Embassy Office Parks REIT	91
8.2	Mindspace Business Parks REIT	96
8.3	Brookfield India Real Estate Trust	100

9. FRACTIONAL OWNERSHIP

9.1	Fractional Ownership in Real Estate	105
9.2	How does fractional ownership work?	106
9.3	Structure of Fractional Real Estate Ownership	107
9.4	Types of Fractional Real Estate Ownership	107
9.5	Valuation of Fractional Ownership Interest	108
9.6	Advantages of Fractional Ownership in Real Estate	110
9.7	Fractional Ownership Vs Timeshare	111

10. GLOBAL FRACTIONAL OWNERSHIP

10.1	Fractional ownership in the USA	112
10.2	Fractional ownership in Singapore	113
10.3	Fractional ownership in Australia	116

10.4 Fractional ownership in London	117
10.5 Summary	118

11. INDIAN FRACTIONAL OWNERSHIP

11.1 Introduction	120
11.2 Properties	120
11.3 Ownership structure	122
11.4 Financing the investment	122
11.5 Regulatory authority	123
11.6 Taxation process	123
11.7 Due diligence process	124
11.8 Fees charged	125
11.9 Documentation	126
11.10 Exit policies	127
11.11 Risks	128
11.12 Indian Fractional Regimes	130

12. BLOCKCHAIN IN REITs AND FO

12.1 What is blockchain?	134
12.2 Blockchain in REIT	135
12.3 Blockchain in Fractional Ownership	140

CHAPTER 1

WHY INVEST IN REAL ESTATE?

1.1 REASONS TO INVEST IN REAL ESTATE

Passive Income

Most people who invest in real estate for a steady cash flow earn it as rental income. It is one of the main reasons which motivates anyone to invest in real estate. This type of passive income depends mainly on the location. Properties in urban cities or towns with good economic interests get higher returns because of high demand. If chosen correctly, the investor can get a steady income which usually rises over time and leads to higher cash flows. With the advent of technology and new services like fractional ownership, passive real estate investing has become less expensive and accessible to investors. Buying various rental properties in different cities can diversify the investor's real estate investment portfolio.

Appreciation of asset value

Historically, it is a proven fact that income-producing real estate investments provide excellent appreciation in value that meet and exceed other types of investment. The property value increases over time as the net operating income rises with increased rent and more effective asset management. It can lead to sale and reinvestment in other properties or provide funds to use for other investments.

Cash flows

Initially, when the real estate is purchased, the cash flow is lower, and the principal reduction on the mortgage is also less. The cash flow increases as the mortgage are paid overtime. It may seem like a forced savings program but yields a greater amount as time goes by and can be a reliable source of income in retirement.

Equity build-up

Another significant advantage of investing in real estate is building equity. As you start paying the mortgage, the principal amount reduces, which in turn builds your equity. As the property's market value increases, the equity of the investor in the property also raises. It enables the investor to take a top-up loan which they can use to invest in other opportunities or renovate the property. With recent changes in guidelines and repo rates, home loans are available at attractive rates, which has made it the best time to invest in real estate.

Inflation hedging

As inflation increases, the buying power of the consumer decreases. An inflation hedge is an investment whose value is expected to increase over time. Real estate investing is one of the great ways to beat inflation. As the prices rise, the rental income and the value of the property also increase. It protects investors from the effects of inflation.

Portfolio diversification

Real estate comes under the category of alternative investments, which include everything from art to physical gold. Usually, real estate has a low correlation with other asset classes. Adding real estate to a portfolio of diversified assets can produce a higher return per unit of risk.

Physical asset

In a world of uncertainty, real estate's tangible nature makes it one of the investors' most reliable options. The market swings may cause some assets which exist only on paper to lose their value within a day. Income-generating real estate is one of those investment classes, which has significant value as a hard asset.

1.2 WHY REAL ESTATE IN COVID'19 CRISIS?

We are in the midst of the uncommon emergency that has brought the economy to a sudden stop. People are looking at opportunities that offer them financial stability, safety and security. Here's why they should look at real estate as a safe option:

1. Once the lockdown is removed, there will be an enormous demand for ready to move-in real estate. As their supply is less, prices will increase.

2. The huge decrease in the Repo rate (75 bps), Reverse Repo rate and CRR by the Reserve Bank of India (RBI) will bring down the borrowing costs for both home buyers and investors.

3. To boost their sales during the lockdown, developers are offering lucrative offers and exciting payment plans. It brings down the property rates, and homebuyers can expect to get deals at almost launch prices.

4. The deadline to avail the CLSS component of the Pradhan Mantri Awas Yojana (PMAY) has now been extended till 31 March 2021 for the MIG category and till 31 March 2022 for LIG/EWS category. This move by the government will create a positive environment for home buyers.

1.3 CONSUMER SENTIMENT SURVEYS

During the lockdown, Consumer Sentiment Surveys were conducted by a few organizations to the opinion about knowing the best asset class for investment amidst COVID-19.

One of the surveys was conducted jointly by NAREDCO & Housing.com Research (**'Concerned, Yet Positive - Real Estate**

Consumer Sentiment Survey'). The other was conducted by ANAROCK Group (**Covid-19 Impact on Indian - Real Estate Consumer Sentiment Survey**). Both the surveys indicated that Real Estate is the best investment option.

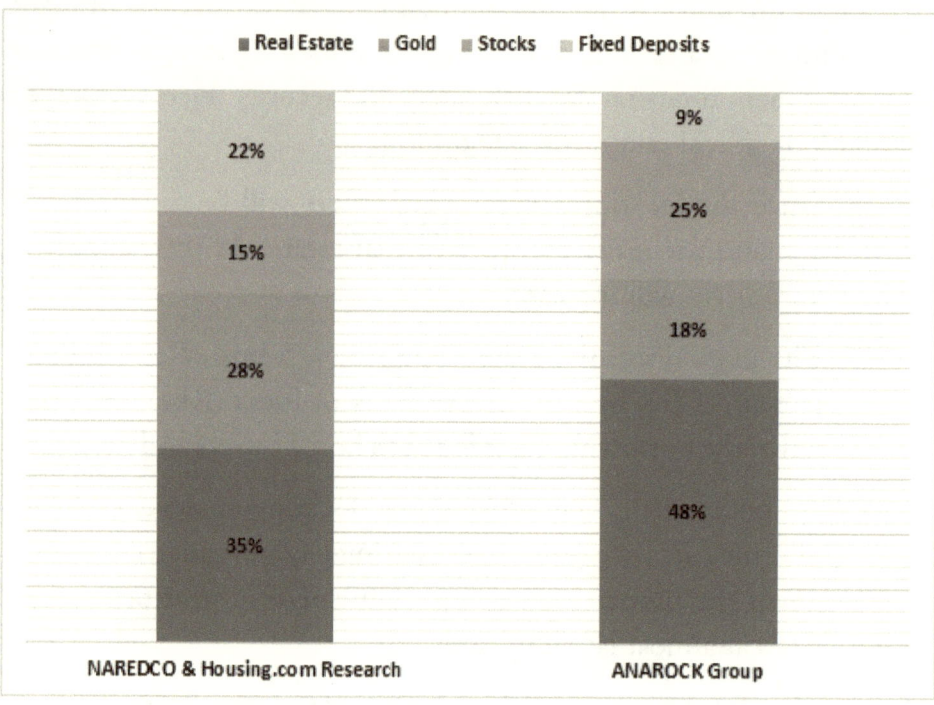

1.4 REAL ESTATE VS OTHER OPTIONS

Real Estate

A Real Estate investment is often a good and reliable investment chance to come up with substantial returns. Real estate creates a regular income flow and provides capital appreciation and benefits like diversification and tax advantage. Returns in Real Estate can be obtained by investment such as capital appreciation, rental income, REITs, online Real Estate platform, etc. The sources of income through investment in this sector are further explained in details in further chapters.

Stocks

A stock market is a place where people trade in bonds, shares and derivatives. SEBI (Securities and Exchange Board of India) regulates India's stock markets and ensures that India's securities markets work in order. The stock exchanges facilitate the trading process. In India, there are two primary stock exchanges: the Bombay Stock Exchange (BSE) and the National Stock Exchange (NSE). The broker is a professional who purchases and sells orders for investors in exchange for a commission.

The two ways to earn through investing in shares are dividends and capital appreciation. Apart from capital gains on shares, investors may expect income in the form of dividends. The companies usually distribute profits to the shareholders by declaring dividends.

Mutual fund

A Mutual fund is a kind of financial vehicle that allows investors to park their money in a range of assets and securities, like equities, debts, money market instruments and liquid assets. Professional fund managers take up the task of managing these mutual funds. They allocate the fund's investments and strive to generate capital gains or income for the fund investors. Since money is pooled from totally different investors toward a fund, the rewards, profits, risks and losses are also shared among them, according to the extent of their investment.

Investors can earn returns from a mutual fund in three ways:

1. Income is earned from dividends on stocks and interest on bonds held in the fund's portfolio. A fund pays almost all of the income it receives over the year to fund owners in the form of a distribution. Funds offer investors a choice to receive a check for distributions or reinvest the earnings and get more shares.

2. If the fund sells securities that have increased in price, the fund has a capital gain. Most funds also pass on these gains to investors in a distribution.

3. If fund holdings increase in price but are not sold by the fund manager, the fund's shares increase in price.

Gold

Gold is one of India's most preferred investments. The reasons why people prefer gold is because of its high liquidity and its inflation-hedging capability. Many families in India pass on gold from one generation to another.

The investment in gold was traditionally made by buying physical gold in coins, bullions, artefacts, or jewellery. However, today, there are more recent gold investments, like gold ETFs (exchange-traded funds) and gold funds. These Gold ETFs are similar to buying an equivalent sum of physical gold but without the hassles of having to store the physical gold. So, the risk of theft/burglary is zero as gold is stored in Demat form. Gold funds involve investing in gold mining companies.

Cash/Savings

Money that is thought of as savings is commonly placed into an interest-earning account where the risk of losing your deposit is shallow. Though you will be able to reap more significant returns with higher-risk investments, like stocks, the concept behind savings is to permit the money to grow slowly with little or no associated risk. The savings can be done in savings accounts through fixed deposits, postal schemes, certificates of deposits (CD) and treasury bills.

Savings allow you to squirrel money away while earning modest, low-risk returns. Due to the wide range of investment vehicles and constantly changing interest rates, a little research can go a long way in determining which will work most challenging for you. Also, emergency money has been essential for the coronavirus crisis, so your sense of how much you should have within easy reach may have changed.

1.5 COMPARISON FACTORS

1. **Appreciation/ROI**

    Real Estate: Real estate has always proved to be one of the best ways of long-term appreciation and to produce a regular monthly income in the form of liquid cash. According to NCREIF, the avg. return on 25-year investment in commercial real estate is 9.4%. While residential and diversified real estate investments average at 10.5%, Real Estate Investment Trusts (REITs) produce an average annual return of 10.5%.

    Stocks: The stock market investing makes sense when it comes to benefits like matching or catch-up contributions. Investing in the share market is very unpredictable, and the returns are often lower than expected. Also, stocks have seen time to time crash due to crises and scams happening in India. Investors lost nearly INR 11 Million crores in the stock markets in a single day as the Bombay Stock Exchange (BSE), SENSEX, and Nifty registered their biggest fall in absolute terms after the WHO's declaration on coronavirus.

    Mutual Funds: Mutual funds differ based on several parameters, such as market caps, risks, etc. Large-caps invest in assets and securities over the long-term; they offer healthy returns against market risks. They are best suited for long-term investors with low-risk appetites. The average return for stock mutual funds, an excellent long-term return (annualized, for ten years or more) is 8%-10%. For bond mutual funds, a superior long-term return would be 4%-5%.

    Gold: Gold investment is worthwhile as it gives inflation-beating results. But the dark side is there is a devaluation of paper currency when gold appreciates. Over a decade, gold delivered negative returns in three out of the last ten calendar years. In the years of 2013, 2014, and 2015, the returns of gold were -4.9%, -8.2% and -6.2%. In the remaining seven years, gold delivered returns ranging between 5.2% in 2017 to 31.7% in 2011. It has produced a return of 11% (in rupees terms), according to data from the World Gold Council (WGC) data as of 9 April 2020.

Cash/Savings: Returns on savings can be achieved by investing in FD offered by small banks or post office schemes. FD are one of the most preferred options as they provide capital safety and guaranteed returns. But a one-year bank fixed deposit (FD) earned a return upwards of 6.5 per cent along with capital safety. Small savings schemes (SSS) offer interest rates that are higher than the ones provided by banks. There are SSS and PPF, which are offering a return of up to 7.9 per cent. There are some schemes for senior citizens which provide a slightly higher rate of interest. But at the end of the day, these savings can be less beneficial than investments in assets.

2. **Leverage**

    Real Estate: The most common way to leverage your money in real estate is with your own money or a mortgage. Leverage works to one's advantage when property values rise. Investors get excellent returns and monthly cash flows by holding onto the leveraged property in the long term.

    Stocks: Stock market leverage can increase your return on investment, but you can lose more money than when buying stock using only your funds.

    Mutual funds: Some types of mutual funds use leverage, and leverage can increase returns, but there are restrictions to maintain mutual fund liquidity.

Gold: A leverage in gold can be a valuable tool in the right circumstances. A considerable amount of flexibility is allowed in Futures contracts and other derivatives. In conclusion, it is best to use enough leverage to generate average returns without using so much leverage to expose excessive risk.

Cash/Savings: Liquid asset secured financing lets you leverage assets in one or more investment accounts without liquidating the investment.

3. **Tax benefits**

   Real Estate: Real estate has structured tax benefits. Some of the details like depreciation, repairs cost, mortgage tax deductions, legal costs and other maintenance costs are considered while computing the tax.

   Stocks: For the capital gains obtained by selling shares held for less than 12 months on stock exchanges, the tax rate is 15%. In cases where the applicable slab tax rate is 10 per cent, you will still have to pay 15 per cent on such short-term capital gains.

   Mutual funds: They are considered more tax-efficient than other types of financial instruments available in the market. ELSS is a different class of funds that are exempt from tax for the INR 1.5 Lakhs limit.

   Gold: Gold also attracts capital gains tax. Any gain obtained in the case of gold deposit certificates is exempted from tax.

   Cash/Savings: Even though fixed deposits comes under 80C investments, the returns you earn are taxable. A 10% TDS is deducted on the FD returns if the total interest exceeds Rs. 10,000 in a financial year. For joint accounts, only the primary account holders can avail of tax benefits.

4. **Risks**

    Real Estate: Real estate capital appreciation makes the buying and holding the best long-term low-risk investments. Meanwhile, the rental property can act as a source of cash flow, giving enough income while the property appreciates.

    Stocks: The stock market is subjected to several risks: Market risk, economic troubles, and inflationary risk. Other risks may stem from the investor himself. Investors who do not diversify their portfolio of stocks or depend on specific stock are at a higher risk.

    Mutual funds: As the saying goes – 'Mutual funds are subject to market risk'. Like most investments, there is risk in mutual funds, and investors could lose money on their investment. An investor investing in mutual funds is liable to market risk, inflation risk, interest rate risk, currency risk and credit risk.

    Gold: In the current crisis, buying gold may seem like a safe way to protect your finances. But unpredictable market forces and scams don't make gold the safest option to invest.

    Cash/Savings: An FD account is a safe place to park your money, where market risks cannot touch the investment or the interest. RBI offers insurance for deposits up to Rs. 1 lakh. So, your money is safe by all means. But having hard cash in large numbers can seem troublesome

5. **Hard assets**

    Real Estate: Real estate property is tangible and has an intrinsic value because of its substance and physical properties.

    Stocks: These are incredibly liquid assets as they can be converted into cash in a short period, even in case of any emergency.

    Mutual funds: Like stocks, mutual funds too are liquid assets.

Gold: Gold is a tangible asset and creates a safe perception to the investors.

Cash/Savings: Hard cash can be termed as tangible assets. But saving in the form of deposits and schemes are liquid assets.

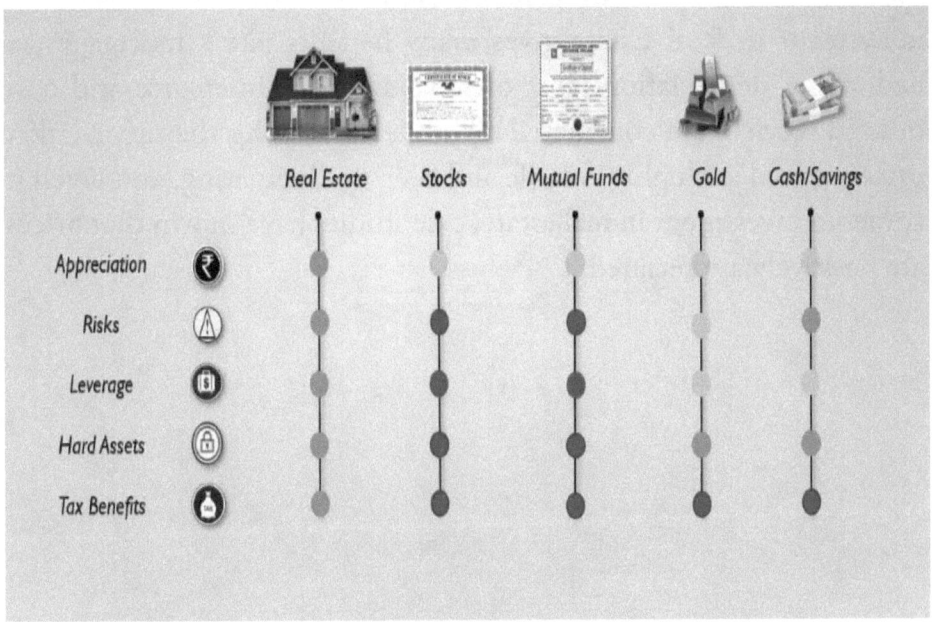

1.6 SUMMARY

The most basic plan of investment is to gain profits. Stocks and Mutual funds generate reliable income. It would take high risks to invest in them to deliver high returns; Real Estate is appealing because it is a tangible asset. In contrast, income generated by real estate investment in rent is regular and keeps up with inflation. We can note from the current crisis that stocks and mutual funds are very volatile and can wipe of crores of investment in a short time. They are sensitive to other economic factors such as monetary policy, regulations, tax revisions, or even changes in the Reserve Bank of India's interest rates. Real estate prices do not fluctuate as sharply and suddenly as stocks. Hence, investment in Real Estate is preferable over stocks and mutual funds.

Whereas considering gold investments, returns from this will not be appreciated more than that of real estate. Also, when it comes to savings and FD's, they don't benefit us with huge returns. Focusing on tax payment, we have to pay the tax directly proportional to the investment made in gold or even on savings/FDs. Whereas investment in Real Estate gives many benefits like a mortgage tax deduction, depreciation, cost of repairs and maintenance and cost of legal services are considered all while calculating the tax. Market prices of gold are highly volatile and keep on fluctuating, and when it comes to investment in real estate, case studies have shown that prices are positively appreciated.

CHAPTER 2

REAL ESTATE AS AN ASSET CLASS

Class

2.1 WHAT IS AN ASSET CLASS?

An asset class is a set of financial instruments with characteristics that can be compared and exhibit similar characteristics in the market place. Some examples of asset classes are Stocks, Bonds, Real estate and Cryptocurrency.

The real estate asset class is broken down into four main property types:

- Residential
- Commercial
- Retail
- Industrial

2.2 RESIDENTIAL ASSET CLASS

Residential real estate deals with providing housing for individuals and families. It is the most common type of asset class about which most people have awareness. There is an assortment of property types that fall under residential real estate. Here's a breakdown of property types:

1. **Single-family homes**

    A single-family home is a residential structure owned and maintained as a single unit and has private access to the street. The facilities such as the swimming pool and heaters are exclusive to the residents. Families who prefer substantial open spaces and plenty of room to spread out opt for single-family homes. Some investors buy the property at a discounted price and renovate it to sell it at a higher price.

Single-family home

2. **Multi-family properties**

A multi-family property is a type of classification where an individual owns each unit, but all the residents jointly own the amenities and common areas. Units are generally stacked on top of each other and are beside each other. The maintenance charges for the amenities such as swimming pools, tennis courts, golf courses are shared among the inhabitants. Most people who prefer a home that has a sense of security and low maintenance choose multi-family properties. It is the most common choice for first-time investors.

Multi-family Properties

3. **Townhouse**

Townhouses, also known as row houses, are single-family homes built beside each other and share common walls. Each unit has its lawn and driveway. It gives the owners the freedom to customize their interior and exterior spaces. These townhouses are usually located inside a gated community with all the luxurious recreational facilities like pool, gym and clubhouse and can be used on a shared basis. A townhouse in a gated community gives you a strong sense of privacy, safety and security.

Townhouses

4. **Vacation homes**

Vacation home usually referred to as second homes, is the type of property used mainly for recreational purposes mostly during vacations. It is usually a fully furnished unit used by the owner only during a particular time of the year. When not being utilized, it may be rented out, which can be a decent source of passive income. Vacation homes are usually seen in cities situated in the coastal region of India.

Vacation Home

5. Co-living spaces

Co-living is the type of housing where people with common interests and values share the living space. It involves sharing facilities like a common kitchen, laundry, and utility space. These facilities are usually provided by the company which manages the co-living space. We can see that the demand for this type of housing is growing in metropolitan cities as single working persons who do not wish to rent a house are opting for co-living spaces to save costs. In the past few years, the demand for student housing has also increased tremendously.

Co-living Spaces

6. Mixed-Use development

Mixed-use development is a type of property that can be used for residential and commercial/retail purposes within a relatively small area. Depending on the size of the land, developers may opt for either horizontal development or vertical development. Most developers choose residential and retail combination because retail attracts more footfalls. Transit-oriented development is also being implemented in some of the metropolitan cities.

Horizontal Mixed-use Development   Vertical Mixed-use Development

2.3 COMMERCIAL ASSET CLASS

Commercial property is a building or a structure that is used for business purposes. This property is exclusively used for business purposes or to provide a workspace. Below is a list of the various types of commercial properties and their subcategories:

1. **Office Spaces**

    Commercial office space is a property utilized by business professionals, tech and finance firms, medical professionals, and many more. Office buildings range from large multi-tenant structures in City Business Districts (CBD) to single-tenant buildings. Standard office space is divided into separate rooms, and it typically includes restrooms and probably a residential-style kitchen. Rents and valuations of offices are influenced by employment growth, a region's economical and productivity rates.

Office Space

2. **Co-working spaces**

Co-working is an arrangement where several workers from completely different firms share an office space that permits cost-saving and convenience by utilizing common infrastructures, such as equipment, utilities, receptionist and custodial services, and some cases, refreshments and parcel acceptance services. Co-working spaces are the best workplace for freelancers and start-ups.

Co-working spaces

3. **Hotel and Lodgings**

   This type of property consists of several individual residential units. Hotels and lodgings provide accommodations and various services to business travellers and tourists and typically include a large commercial kitchen or on-site restaurant. Some units, however, may be suites that have multiple rooms, a kitchen or a bar, and possibly also an in-room Jacuzzi or spa.

   Hotels

4. **Restaurants**

   A restaurant is an asset wherein it uses its resources to run its operations and serve its guests. This property will vary in size and complexity. It will generally include a large kitchen with commercial appliances, a storage room or pantry, a refrigerated space, an office, a dining area, and public restrooms.

Restaurants

5. **Self-Storage units**

Self-storage facilities are commercial properties that rent space to tenants either on a monthly or long-term basis. These spaces can range in size from lockers to rooms, containers, and even outdoor space. It provides customers with safe, secure, and handy accessible facilities, where they can rent a dedicated room and store their personal and household items and corporate goods.

Self-Storage units

6. **Special Purpose**

    Particular purpose commercial real estate consists of property designed for a specific use. Some special-purpose property examples include amusement parks, schools, railroad stations or bus terminals, religious facilities, Self-storage facilities, golf courses, bowling alleys, sports arenas, parking structures, government buildings, theatres.

2.4 RETAIL ASSET CLASS

Retail real estate consists of companies that develop and manage properties for shopping and entertainment purposes. It is a highly desirable asset class for investors as it attracts huge footfalls. The types of retail real estate are:

1. **Malls**

    Malls are large indoor spaces which consist of a variety of retail stores, services, and parking area. They are usually anchored by department stores and draw customers regularly from surrounding neighbourhoods. Malls are considered to be one of the main drivers of the retail industry in India.

    Mall

2. **Lifestyle centres**

   Lifestyle centres are shopping centres that have high-end retail stores. These are situated in a single building or a set of connected buildings which have parking facilities. They can be referred to as malls without department stores. Located usually in affluent areas, they attract upscale customers. They also have leisure amenities such as gaming centres, restaurants and movie theatres.

   Lifestyle Centre

3. **Factory outlets**

   Factory outlets, also referred to as outlet stores, are retail stores partially/fully owned by manufacturers. They are a way for the companies to sell slightly damaged goods, overproduced stock and unsold merchandise. They are typically located next to the factories where the products are manufactured.

Factory Outlet

4. **Power centres**

Power centres are outdoor shopping centres that have multiple big-box retailers. They also have small retailers and other businesses. These units surround a common parking area which is shared by all of them. Power centres are meant to make big-box stores more visible to the consumers.

Power Centre

5. **Neighbourhood centres**

   Neighbourhood Centres are shopping centres that offer accessible shopping facilities for the consumers' daily needs in the surrounding areas. The tenants are usually department stores and other small businesses.

   Neighbourhood Centre

6. **Convenience centres**

   Convenience centres are small shopping centres that have stores that sell services and other convenience goods. The tenants typically include minimarket, drugstore, salon and dry cleaners. The prices in the convenience centres are usually a bit on the higher side.

Convenience Centre

2.5 INDUSTRIAL ASSET CLASS

Industrial real estate is usually located in suburban areas with access to major highways or air transportation systems. These industrial properties are typically stable, longer-term investments. The properties may range from warehouses to large-scale e-commerce sorting facilities to specific tenant-driven uses. Broadly they are classified as:

1. **Manufacturing Facility**

    Manufacturing sites are the property where goods are produced and assembled. It is categorised as a heavy manufacturing facility or a light assembly facility depending on goods produced. Heavy manufacturing commercial real estate properties typically comprise thousands to even hundreds of thousands of square feet to accommodate heavy equipment and production lines. These facilities are customised for specific owners and tenants.

Manufacturing Plant

2. **Warehouse/ Storage & Distribution**

These buildings are used for the general storage and distribution of goods. Depending on the type of products being stored, the property's size can have an extensive square foot range. The structure's layout tends to be an open space, where the ceiling is open to the roof's interior design. Warehousing primarily constitutes a critical link in the chain that connects the manufacturer to the eventual consumer.

Warehouse

3. **Flex Space**

   Flex Spaces are industrial, commercial properties that are designed for diverse use. It is a building that combines more than one use in a single facility. The identifying factor for this property is the amount of office space. There is always more office space in flex buildings than in any other types of industrial properties. The site typically comprises at least 30% office space, as well as space for production. Examples of flex space include research and development facilities, data centres, and showrooms.

   Flex Space

CHAPTER 3

HOW TO INVEST IN REAL ESTATE

3.1 PRIMARY VS SECONDARY MARKET

Before any investors start investing, they need to know the differences between primary and secondary markets.

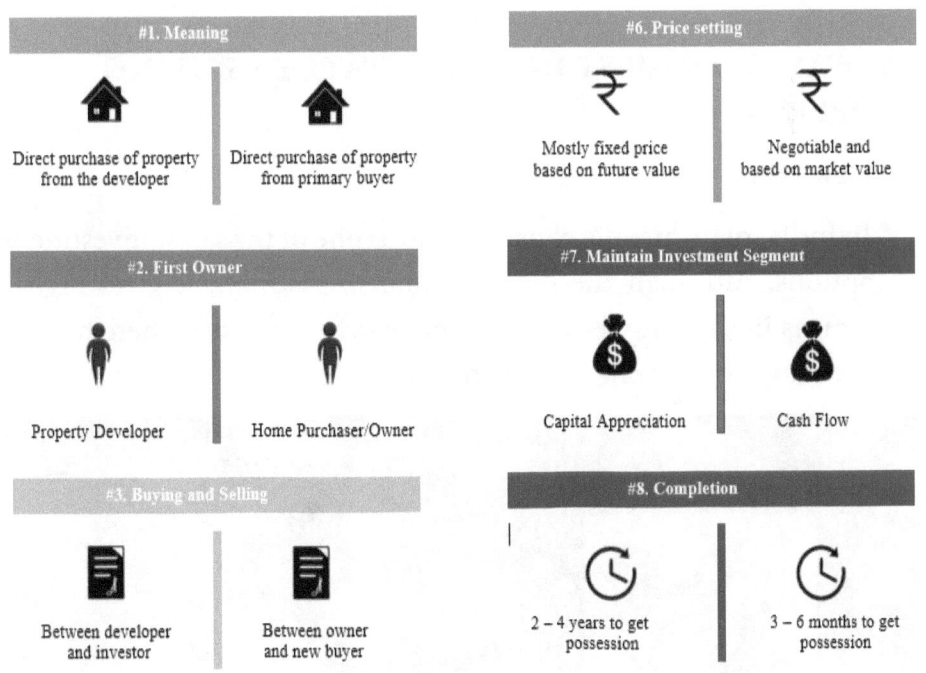

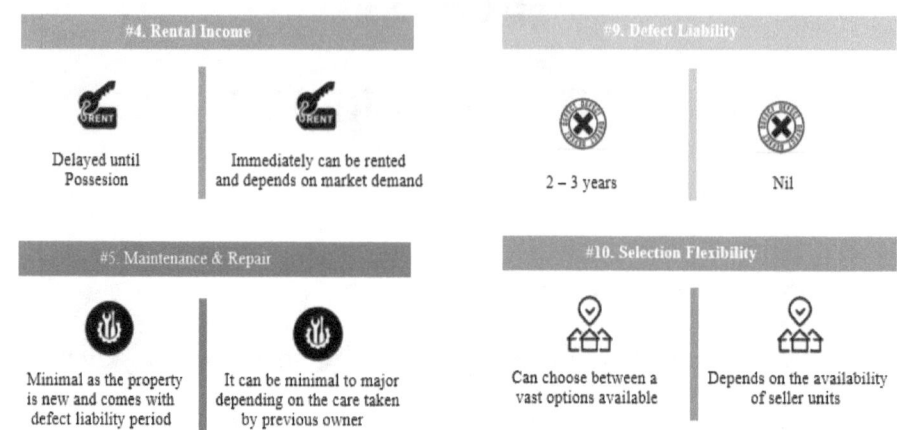

3.2 WAYS TO INVEST IN REAL ESTATE BY BUYING PROPERTY

1. **Raw land**

   In India, many people consider land as one of the safest investment options. Although the initial capital size is high, it gives higher returns in the long term. Over the past few decades, there haven't been any volatile changes in the land price.

Source: AZ Quotes

Benefits of investing in the land are:

- As the supply is limited and the chances of creating more are nearly impossible, land always has an ever-growing demand.
- Maintaining a plot of land is very easy as it does not require any repairs or renovations. Investors can purchase land and need not worry about its regular upkeep.
- Investors have the flexibility of deciding a land's usage policy. Within the government regulations, they can choose to construct an income-generating asset or build a property for their use.
- People buying an under-construction property may have to wait for some time to take possession of it. Purchasing land gives investors immediate possession.

Different methods of investing in the land are:

- Holding it until the price gets appreciated
- Building a property and selling it later
- Giving it for a long-term lease to businesses

Few factors to be considered before investing in the land are:

- Location
- Zoning regulations
- Size and shape of the plot
- Nearby infrastructure
- History of the property

2. **House flipping**

House flipping is the process of purchasing an income-generating asset, increasing its value and reselling for a higher price. It is a short-term strategy that is used in property investing to gain quick profits. People with good knowledge of landscaping and design can get into the business of flipping houses.

House flipping can be done in two ways:

- Buy a property in a rapidly growing market, hold it for a few months and sell it for a profit.

- Buy a property at a relatively low price, make some repairs and renovations and sell it for a higher price.

    The 70 per cent rule of house flipping states that a buyer should pay only 70 per cent of the ARV (After Repair Value) of the property minus the repair costs to the seller.

Source: southernbelleproperties.com

3. **Vacation property**

    Vacation homes can be fantastic investments as homeowners could earn income by renting out a house or even just a room on a short-term basis, especially if the property is in an area that's a well-known tourist destination. These homes have a natural appeal as a rental because they typically are used by their owners for a few weeks throughout the year.

Vacation homes are highly in demand in India. People nowadays prefer to stay in vacation property such as farmhouse and villas, which provide the flexibility of a stay at a low cost over the hotel rooms.

The types of vacation homes are:

- Mountain lodge
- Woodland cabin
- Beach house
- Lakeside retreat
- City townhouse

Source: rent-holiday-homes.com

4. **Co-living spaces & Student housing**

    Co-living is a housing concept where users, usually not from a single-family, share a living space. The residents of a co-living space generally have similar interests, intentions and values. These are mainly being opted by the millennial crowd who migrate to cities for employment/educational opportunities.

    The co-living format has been in India for the past few decades in paying guest accommodations (PGs) and institution run hostels. These unorganised arrangements are not governed by any rules and do not provide their residents with basic amenities. Most of the PGs and hostels impose irrelevant restrictions, which makes the living experience very uncomfortable.

    In recent years, there has been an increase in companies offering organized co-living spaces in metropolitan cities. They have comfortable living spaces and provide facilities like Wi-Fi and housekeeping. Users can also save a lot of money in brokerage costs as most of the areas have online websites through which the transactions can be completed. The residents have complete autonomy to choose their roommates and do not have any entry or exit barriers.

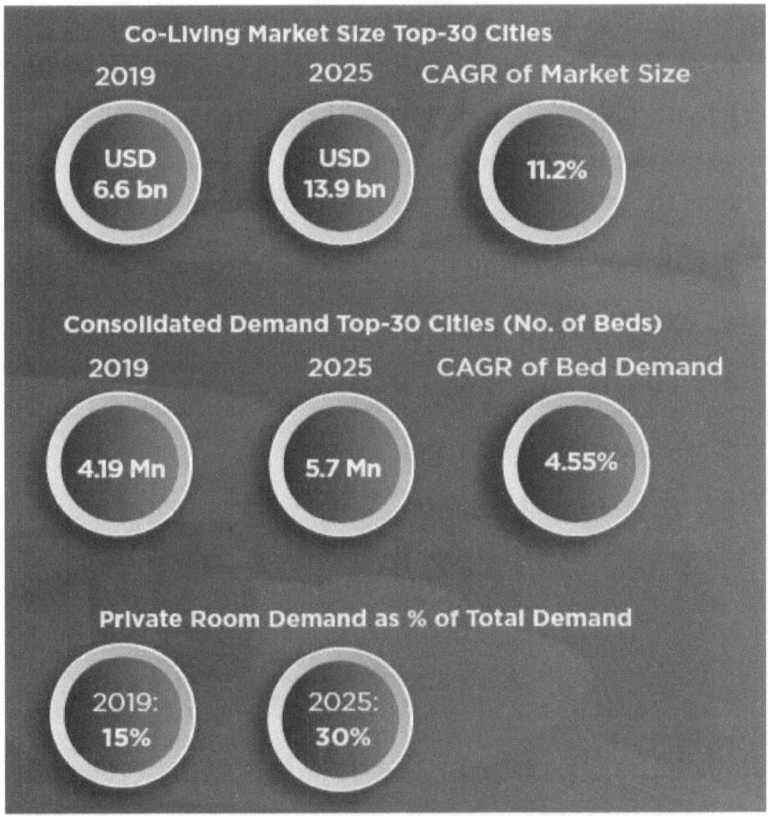

Source: Cushman & Wakefield Report

Some of India's co-living spaces are Zolo Stays, CoHo, Oyo Life, NestAway, Stanza Living, Oxfordcaps and Placio.

5. **Commercial Properties**

For commercial property investment, the investor can look at offices spaces, retail buildings, or warehouses. Commercial real estate (CRE) succeeds as an investment by producing rental income from a tenant or multiple tenants. This rental income becomes cash flow or revenue for the equity owner of the property. For CRE that functions through a fund, this rental income often reaches investors' hands in cash or dividend distributions. Commercial asset investment is high-risk yet high-reward real estate. Revenue generated from renting space to professional tenants or businesses is usually higher than that from the residential market. The lease contract in commercial buildings is longer than residential, guaranteeing a regular cash flow for a more extended period.

Benefits of investing in commercial property are:

- Higher returns
- Longer lease time
- Consistent and regular returns
- Professional tenants

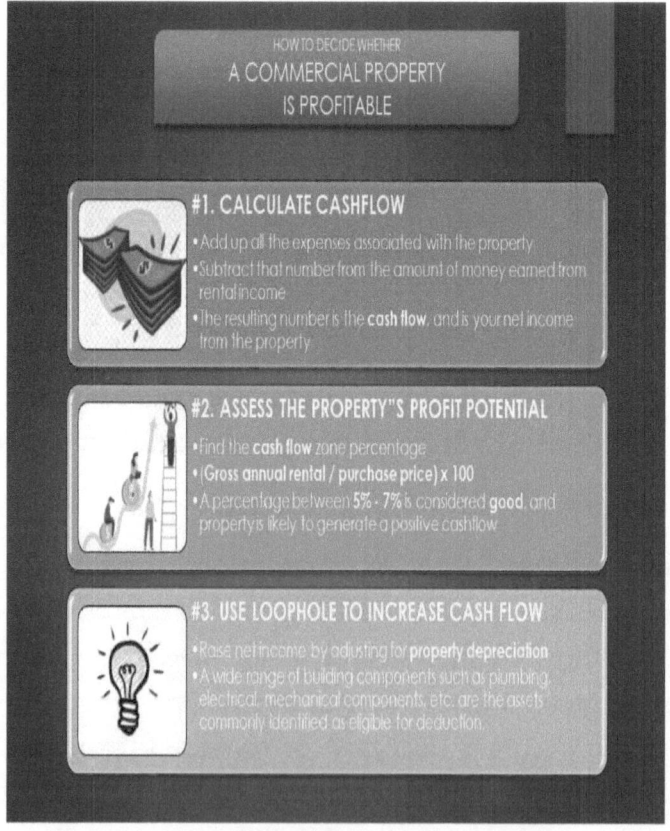

Source: westwoodnetlease.com

6. Rental Properties

The majority of residential property financial gains come in the form of basic rent. You could purchase a property and rent out any room or apartment to tenants. The tenants pay a fixed amount per month, going up with inflation and acting as rental income. A property rented in CBD or near educational Institutions always fetches a good rental income. Setting the right rent for the property is always important. Following factors should be considered to set suitable rent:

If property is bought recently, know the rent set by previous owner

Research the market for the rent charged by comparable properties in neighborhood.

Any specific feature of the property that set it apart from other rentals.

Amenities and facilities, you will provide to the tenants.

Calculate your costs including loan installments, taxes, etc. before setting the rent.

7. Fractional Ownership

Fractional ownership is a new concept booming in the Indian market. Several small investors pool in money to buy a valued commercial or residential property. The rents generated from the property are split among the investors based on the shares of investment in the property.

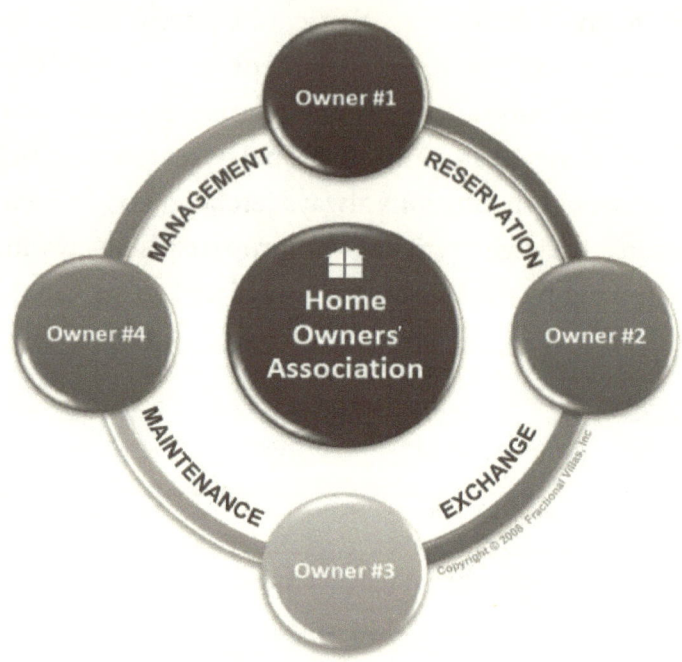

Source: fractionalvillas.com

Some of the Fractional Ownership companies in India through which investment can be made are Strata, FRACSN, Propertyshare, Share Acre, hBits and RealX.

3.3 WAYS TO INVEST IN REAL ESTATE WITHOUT BUYING PROPERTY

1. **REITs**

   Real Estate Investment Trust (REIT) is a vehicle that makes investments in a portfolio of real estate properties. The types of income-generating real estate that a REIT may invest in include office buildings, warehouses, shopping centres, hotels and hospitals. In general, REITs are classified into three types, namely

Equity REITs, Mortgage REITs and Hybrid REITs. The revenue generated by the REITs in rental income, interest income and capital gains is distributed to the shareholders (also referred to as unit holders) in dividends.

India's first listed REIT, Embassy Office Parks, was launched in April 2019. It is a joint venture between Embassy Group and private equity investor Blackstone group. This REIT portfolio consists of office parks and buildings in Mumbai, Bangalore, Pune and National Capital Region (NCR).

2. **MBSs**

A Mortgage-Backed Security (MBS), also called a mortgage bond, is a type of debt instrument made up of loans, usually home and other real estate loans, which have similar characteristics. The two kinds of MBSs are Pass-through MBS and Collateralized Mortgage Obligation (CMO).

Structure of MBS

Source: Invesco

The loans are purchased by financial institutions (government or private agencies), which package them into MBSs to be sold to investors. The selling of loans allows the banks to transfer the credit default risk to investors. The institutions which issue the MBSs act as intermediaries in collecting monthly interest payments and principal payments from the borrowers and passing them onto the unit holders proportionately.

3. **REMFs**

    Real Estate Mutual Funds (REMFs) are sectoral mutual funds that invest in units of various REITs, shares of listed real estate companies and direct purchase of income-producing real estate units. People who are not interested in buying properties can invest in REMFs.

    Some of the features of Real Estate Mutual Funds are:

    - **Long-term investment:** It takes time for getting decent returns from REMFs as it takes time for properties to be developed and sold.

    - **Small investment sizes**: There is no minimum size of the initial investment. Investors can start from a small capital size and increase the size later.

    - **High liquidity factor:** REMFs give flexibility to the investors to sell their funds when the market is up and get higher capital gains

    - **Diversified portfolio:** Investors benefit from investing in varied types ranging from commercial projects to residential rental properties.

    - **Minimal Effort:** REMFs are managed by fund managers who are well experienced in planning the investments and taking care of all the legalities.

REMFs are purchased through investment companies or online platforms. Investors gain returns through dividends and capital appreciation. Some of the REMFs in India are Aditya Birla Real Estate Fund, HDFC Property Fund, Birla Sun Life Global Real Estate Fund and Secura India Real Estate Fund.

4. **REIT ETFs**

    Exchange-traded funds invest in various asset classes like stocks, bonds, mutual funds and commodities. Securities. The provider of an ETF sells the shares, which can be traded on all major stock exchanges. REIT ETFs is the type of exchange-traded funds that invest in the shares of REITs. The majority of the REIT ETFs own shares in equity-REITs. Through a single investment, buyers can earn access to stakes in multiple REITs.

5. **MICs**

    Mortgage Investment Corporation is a company that lends money for purchasing real estate properties. Investors can buy the shares of the MICs, which enables them to invest in a diversified portfolio. A MIC portfolio may consist of a wide variety, from home loans to commercial property loans. The MIC's interest and principal payments are distributed to the investors in dividends after deducting operating expenses. The investors can choose to take the dividend or reinvest it to get additional shares of the MIC.

6. **REIGs (Real Estate Investment Groups)**

    Real Estate Investment Groups (REIGs) are an entity that carries its business by investing in realty. These groups may prefer to buy, renovate, sell, or finance properties to earn profits. They commonly buy a property and sell the units to investors while taking care of that property's administration and maintenance. REIGs earn their revenues in interest and rental incomes, which are distributed to the investors in dividends.

7. **Hard money loans**

   If one doesn't like to deal with the property hustle but want to earn, they can use this strategy wherein you can lend a hard money loan directly to a real estate investor. The income from hard money loans is in the form of interest and principal payments. The returns are usually good because of high-interest rates.

8. **Share markets**

   Like a regular share market, one can also invest in realty stocks that are publicly traded. Companies project pipeline, land bank, balance sheet strength should be checked while choosing the share. The publicly traded real estate companies pay out their earnings to the investors in the form of dividends. When the share prices increase over the long-term, they can be sold for good capital gain.

9. **Private equity**

   Private equity funds are a passive investment in which the investors pool money together and make investments in property markets. These funds are operated by the firms or limited liability partnership by the management group. Investment requires upfront capital. Investors buying equity in a company are entitled to ownership rights. They get a proportional share of the profit.

CHAPTER 4

SOURCES OF INCOME IN REAL ESTATE

4.1 INCOME FROM PHYSICAL INVESTMENTS

Real estate investors earn revenues from physical investments in the following ways:

- Capital Appreciation
- Rental Income

Capital Appreciation

Capital appreciation is defined as the increase in the value of investment assets, for example, real estate or stock, that makes them worth more than what they were at the time of purchase.

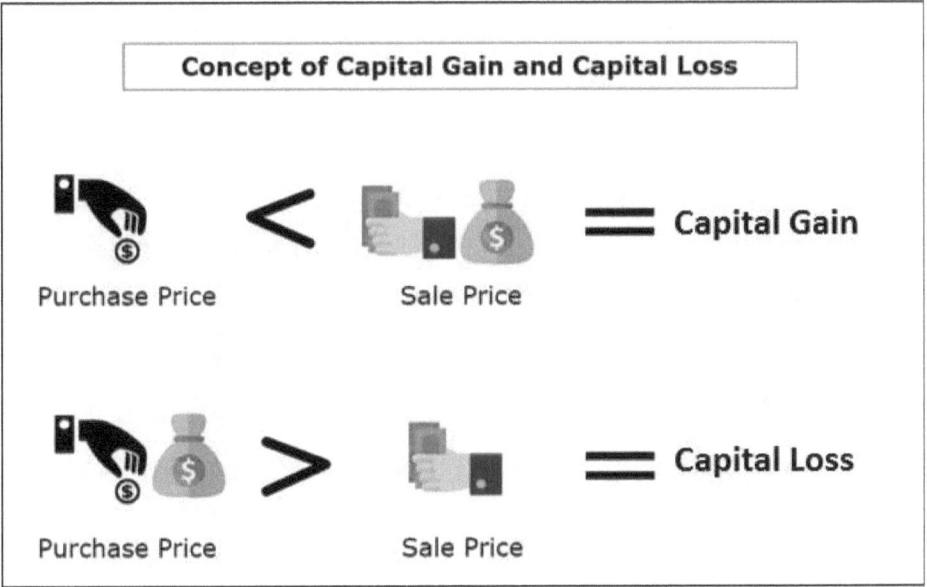

Source: Business Standard

Capital Appreciation in real estate happens in two scenarios:

1. The property value has increased over some time.
2. When a property is bought at a relatively lower price, renovated and then sold at a higher price. Investors use this strategy for quick returns.

Some of the factors which influence the property prices are:

1. **Supply and demand**

    When the demand for a specific type of property, like residential, in a particular geographical location increases and the supply of that property type is not increasing as fast as the demand in that location, the prices tend to grow.

2. **Borrowing costs**

    When the borrowing cost increases, the demand decreases as the number of people who can afford to buy a property decreases. Likewise, when the cost of borrowing decreases, affordability increases which lead to higher demand for property purchase.

3. **Inflation**

    Inflation causes the value of money to reduce, leading to an increase in the price of land, construction materials, and labour. It leads to a rise in construction costs, which in turn increases property prices.

4. **Market developments**

    Some market developments that impact real estate prices are the emergence of new office complexes, new infrastructure projects, shopping malls, educational institutions, and government regulations like zoning restrictions and tax systems changes.

5. **Population growth**

   Population growth in a city leads to an increase in property demand, especially in the housing sector. It also increases the need for infrastructure facilities like public transport.

Rental Income

It is known as the amount of money collected by a landlord from a tenant or group of tenants for the use of a particular space. Most businesses that lack funds or credit standing to purchase their premises can consider the cost of paying rental income periodically that is typically done monthly.

Thumb rule of Rental Income:

The 1 per cent rule is used to determine if the monthly rent earned from an investment property will exceed the property's monthly mortgage payment. The rule's purpose is to ensure that the rental pay earned from the property is more than, or if nothing else, equivalent to the home loan instalment or mortgage payment.

The 2 per cent rule suggests that a rental property is a good investment if the money from rent each month is equal to or higher than 2% of the purchase price.

The 1% and 2% rules for rental properties are valid only at the initial phase of evaluating real estate investments. Utilize the 1 per cent rule as the pre-screening instrument. On the off chance that those numbers meet the standard practice, utilize the 2 per cent rule as a subsequent screening tool. This tool will help evaluate a property's cash flow potential.

Some of the factors that influence rental income are:

1. **Location**

   Location is the most critical factor affecting rental rates for investment property and real estate in general. It establishes a baseline rental rate, overall demand and the target market. Property should have easy access to roads, metro and railway stations, and other physical infrastructures to ensure a smooth inflow of rental income.

2. **Maintenance cost**

   Depending on the property's age, size and quality of construction, and the amenities that accompany it, money has to be shell out for the maintenance costs. If a property is well-maintained, there is a higher chance that it will stay occupied and generate good income for an extended time.

3. **Vacancy rate**

   The vacancy has a direct effect on rental income. The longer the property is vacant, the lower the gross rent collected, and the less valuable a property will be to an investor.

4. **Infrastructure**

   The property that is well connected to entertainment hubs, medical facilities, educational institutions, retail markets and business centres, and other day-to-day facilities helps value the same value escalation.

5. **Affordability**

   It is a relationship between interest rates, property prices and wages. If any of the above three variables reach their maximum level, the investors find it harder to afford to get onto the property ladder and end up renting a property.

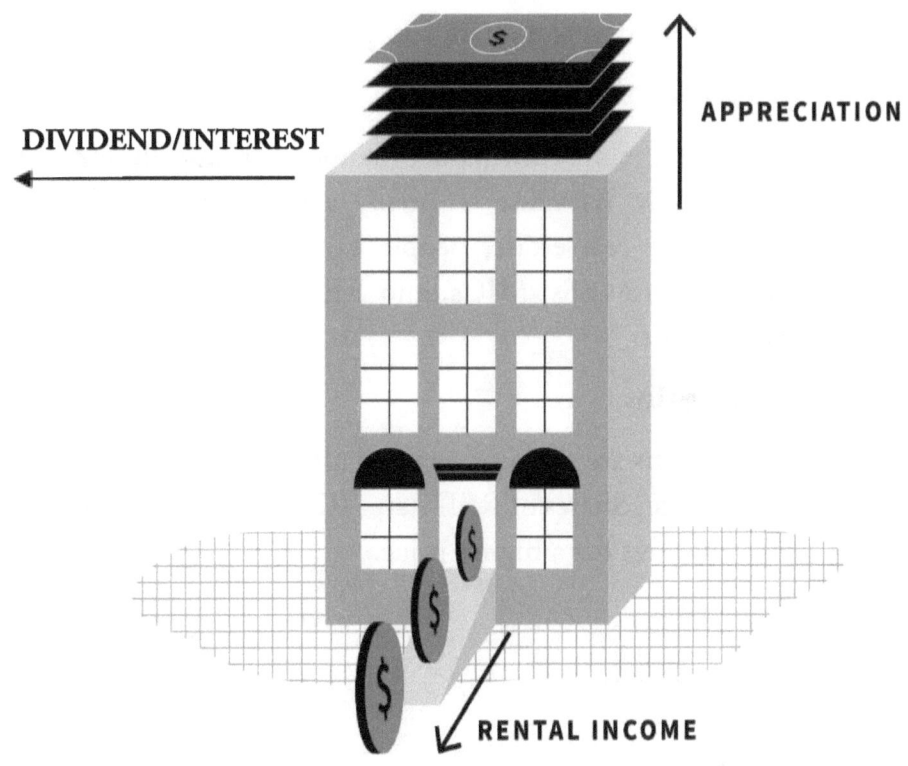

Source: Fundrise

4.2 INCOME FROM NON-PHYSICAL INVESTMENTS

Buying a property isn't the only way to invest in real estate. There are many financial instruments through which investors can invest their money into real estate and get good returns. Income from non-physical investments can be in dividends, interest payments, principal payments, and capital gains.

- **Dividends**

    Dividends are defined as the distribution of earnings to the shareholders in the form of cash or stocks. Most companies usually disburse dividends on an annual basis. In real estate, dividend income is obtained from investing in REITs, REIT ETFs, and listed real estate companies' stocks.

- **Interest & Principal payments**

    Interest is the amount paid to lender periodically for using their money. Its value is usually a percentage of the loan amount. In real estate, people earn interest income from investing in MBSs, MICs, and REIGs and lending money to developers.

- **Capital gains**

    Capital gains are the profit gained after selling the assets for a higher price. Shares of REITs and REIT ETFs can be sold on stock markets for a higher price.

CHAPTER 5

REAL ESTATE INVESTMENT TRUSTS (REITS)

5.1 OVERVIEW

Real Estate Investment Trust (REIT) is a vehicle that makes investments in a portfolio of real estate properties or lends money to real estate companies that own properties. Investors who wish to access real estate can invest in REIT units without directly holding the physical property. REITs usually invest in commercial properties, which generate a steady source of income.

REITs were initially started in the United States of America after introducing a public law named Cigar Excise Tax Extension of 1960 by President Dwight D. Eisenhower. Over the years, the REIT concept has been implemented in more than 35 countries worldwide.

REITs are one of the best investment options for looking for steady cash flows and good long-term appreciation. They give the consistent income that originates from owning and renting properties, yet with the advantage of a typical stock's liquidity.

5.2 STRUCTURE OF A REIT

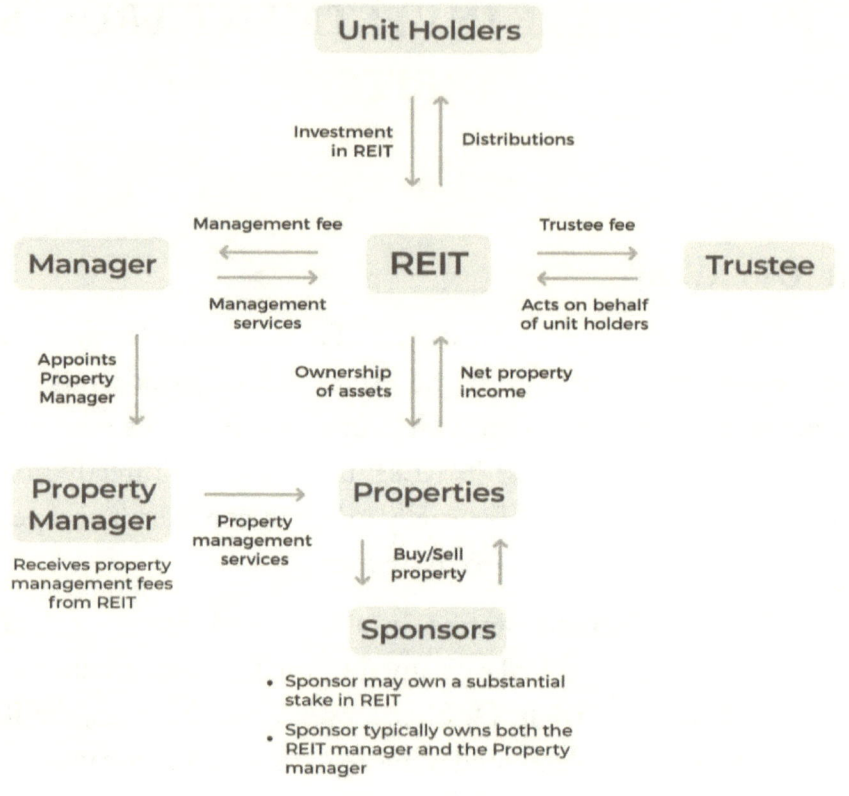

Source: moneysense

Unitholders: Unitholders are investors who own the units of the REIT. They may be individuals or organizations. They earn income through dividend pay-outs or from the sale of their shares.

Trustees: Trustees act on behalf of shareholders. These trustees are responsible for ensuring compliance with regulatory requirements and protecting the rights of shareholders.

REIT Managers: They are responsible for framing the investment policies and strategies, buying and selling properties, redressing investor grievances and setting the dividend policies. They are appointed by the board of directors of the REIT.

Properties: The properties that a REIT owns may include office buildings, residential complexes, shopping centres, hotels, healthcare facilities, data centres, cell towers, industrial estates and warehouses.

Property managers: REIT managers appoint property managers. Their duties include managing day-to-day operations, renting out the asset as per management's strategy, enforcing the terms and conditions, collecting rental income from tenants and providing monthly financial reports to REIT managers.

Sponsors: Sponsors are the owners of the assets that are injected into a REIT's portfolio. They also own a substantial stake in the REIT.

According to the National Association of Real Estate Investment Trusts (NAREIT), a company qualifies as a REIT when the company:

- Invest a minimum of 75% of total assets in real estate, cash, or U.S. Treasuries
- Derive a minimum of 75% of gross income from rents, interest on mortgages that finance the real property, or real estate sales
- Pay a minimum of 90% of taxable income in the form of shareholder dividends annually
- Be an entity that's taxable as a corporation
- Be managed by a board of directors or trustees
- Have a minimum of 100 shareholders after its first year of existence
- Have no more than 50% of its shares held by five or fewer individuals

5.3 HOW DOES A REIT WORK?

After a company gets recognized as a REIT, it releases units that investors can purchase. Each unit represents partial ownership of the pool of assets owned by the company. After getting funds from investors, REITs use them to buy investments or loans to other real estate companies.

How these REITs earn their revenues are through:

- Rental income from leasing its properties to multiple companies
- Interest income from lending to other real estate companies
- Capital gains from the sale of assets at higher prices

After deducting the operating expenses, REITs distribute almost 90% of the income to their investors in dividends.

5.4 TYPES OF REITS

REITs can be classified based on two factors:

a) investment holdings

b) market type.

REITs can be classified into three types based on their investment holdings.

Equity REIT

Equity REITs invest in real estate through the acquisition, development and sale of income-generating properties. In most scenarios, equity REITs also manage and operate their properties. The revenue is generated from rental income and capital gains from the sale of assets.

Mortgage REIT

Mortgage REITs (mREITs) invest exclusively in debt. They lend money to real estate companies through direct lending or the purchase of Mortgage-backed securities (MBSs). The earnings are mainly from interest and principal payments from borrowers.

Hybrid REIT

Hybrid REITs park their funds by investing in both equity and debt real estate investments. The income generated is in the form of rents, interests and principal payments and through capital gains.

Depending on the market type, REITs can be classified into three types:

Publicly traded REITs

Publicly traded REITs are registered with regulatory organizations and list their shares on stock markets just like any other public listed companies. The shares of these are most liquid as they can be traded quickly and do not have any minimum holding period. These REITs are also highly transparent as they publish their financial statements and operations data regularly.

Public non-traded REITs

These REITs are registered with the regulatory bodies bit do not list their shares on stock exchanges. Investors can buy these shares from authorised agents. The shares of public non-traded REITs offer low liquidity as they cannot be traded through secondary markets.

Private REITs

These REITs are not registered with government regulatory boards. They are mostly sold only to institutional investors.

5.5 HOW TO INVEST?

The different ways of investing in REITs are:

- The shares of a listed REITs can be traded through stock exchanges.
- For non-listed REITs, the shares can be sold and purchased through management companies or agents.
- Investments in REITs can also be made by purchasing shares of REIT ETFs or REIT Mutual funds that invest in multiple REITs' securities and derivatives.

Investors earn income from dividends. Dividends are usually in the form of cash payments which may be paid monthly, quarterly, biannually, or annually.

If the investors want to exit a REIT investment, they can list their shares on stock exchanges or sell them through brokers.

5.6 ADVANTAGES OF INVESTING IN REITS

Ease of Investing

The initial investment size is low, unlike buying a property which requires a lot of capital. REITs give retail investors a chance to invest in income-producing assets like commercial and office properties.

Diversification

Diversification adds stability to an investment portfolio as the risk spreads over various asset classes. Most people find it difficult to add real estate to their portfolio because of high costs and maintenance burdens. Investors can start investing in REITs with small amounts and need not worry about the assets' upkeep.

Liquidity

Selling a physical property requires a lot of effort and time. But the shares of a REIT are traded on stock exchanges. Investors can sell their units whenever they want.

Professionally managed

Professional fund managers manage REITs. The design investment strategies in such a way that investors can get maximum benefits. The chance of making an erroneous decision is meagre as these managers are highly skilled and experienced.

Low volatility

Compared to equity markets, REITs are less volatile as property prices and rental income do not fluctuate drastically. Also, the share prices of REITs have a low correlation to that of other asset classes.

CHAPTER 6

GLOBAL REITS

6.1 INTRODUCTION

Globally, Real Estate Investment Trust (REIT) markets multiply, and total market capitalization has surpassed approximately US $1.7 trillion. Nearly 40 countries have adopted the US-based REITs approach. This regime's growth has happened over a decade, with several countries offering it as an investment vehicle and new entrant countries adopting this platform. The REITs have become better understood and more widely accepted worldwide as an investor-friendly and tax-efficient tool for real estate investment.

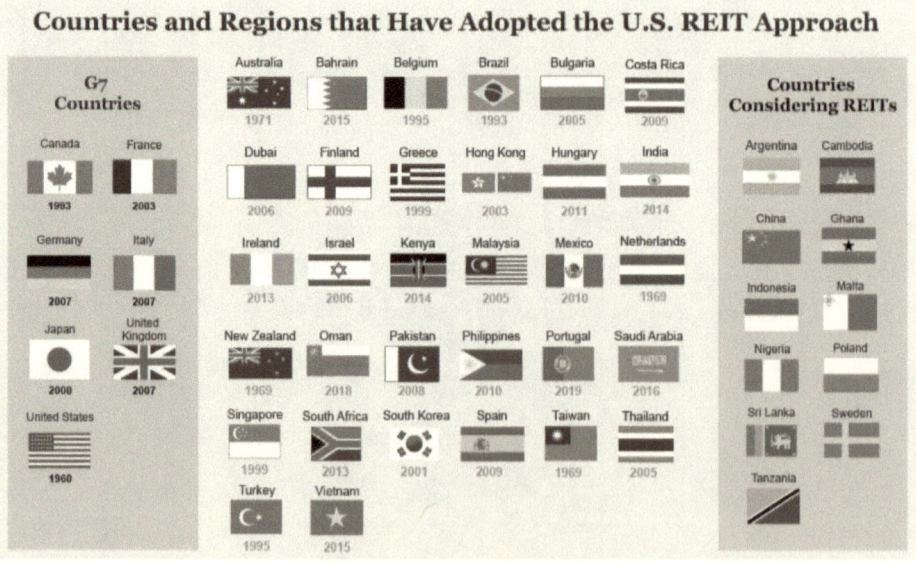

Source: Nareit

It is estimated that all REITs own approximately $3 trillion in gross assets. In which Public REITs account for $2 trillion. (Nareit, data as of January 2020). Four hundred seventy-seven listed real estate companies are included in the FTSE ERPA/Nareit Global Real Estate Index. $1.4 trillion is the total equity capitalization of the FTSE Nareit All REITs Index, including mREITs. Listed REITs account for 81% of the total market capitalization. Non-US constituents represent 52% of the total market capitalization.

6.2 REIT INDEX AND ORGANIZATIONS

National Association of Real Estate Investment Trust (NAREIT)

NAREIT is the worldwide representative voice of REITs. It is an American trade organization for REITs and promotes similar real estate companies around the world.

Nareit is the worldwide representative voice for REITs. It is a member of the Real Estate Equity Securitization Alliance (REESA). REESA is a global equity investment alliance in real estate on a securitized basis. REESA includes members such as the Asian Pacific Real Estate Association (APREA), the Association for Real Estate Securitization (ARES), the British Property Federation (BPF), the European Public Real Estate Association (EPRA), the Property Council of Australia (PCA,), the Real Property Association of Canada (Realpac) and Nareit.

European Public Real Estate Association (EPRA)

The EPRA is the trade association of publicly listed real estate companies or REIT in Europe. They work to promote investments in REITs in Europe and to encourage best practice around the industry. EPRA index is the most common index for the REITs, and the global listed property market is the FTSE EPRA/Nareit Global Real Estate Index Series. It was jointly incorporated by the index provider FTSE Russell,

Nareit and the European Public Real Estate Association (ERPA). It represents the performance of real estate equities around the world. Many institutional investors use this index, fund managers, to manage Real Estate investment globally. It includes both REITs and non-REIT listed property companies and contains both the Developed Markets and Emerging Markets Indices.

Asian Public Real Estate Association (APREA)

APREA is a non-profit industry trade group of Asian REITs. Its goals are to promote real estate investments, promote REITs' interest, and represent the industry to governments in the region.

The **GPR/ APREA Composite Index** is an Asia-Pacific index that tracks the performance of listed real estate securities and REITs across 14 Asia-Pacific countries and eight sectors over multiple time horizons. Global Property Research (GPR) is APREA's listed Index partner. Asia Pacific Real Estate Association (APREA) is an Asian trade group that focuses on cross border real estate investment across AsiaPac.

6.3 STAGES OF REITS GLOBALLY

Worldwide there are almost 40 REITs markets, including all G7 countries. Since 2011, ten new regimes have been established (Bahrain, Hungary, India, Ireland, Kenya, Oman, Portugal, Saudi Arabia, South Africa, Vietnam), and new entrants' countries are on the verge to introduce this regime. Many of the REITs legislations are in the beginning phase of the organisation and progressing towards the growth stage.

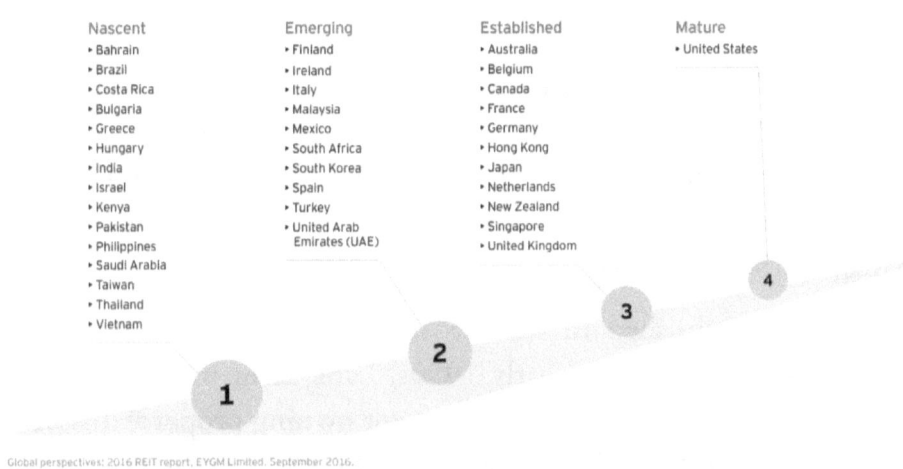

Source: Global perspective: 2016 REIT report, EYGM limited

Ernst & Young Global Limited (EY) has conducted a REIT jurisdiction maturity assessment. They have categorised REIT markets based on their evolution and common themes and grouped them as per their growth stages. As per the report, US REIT, established in 1960, is the most matured market. Following this, Australia and the UK are heading closer to being considered mature markets.

The countries categorised as established markets are in this investment portfolio from the 70s to early 2000s and have developed a fully functional market. Jurisdictions like Ireland, Mexico, and Spain will be considered established shortly, while Finland and South Africa are on the elevation cusp. The jurisdictions under emerging markets had been established over the past decade in which some regimes are maturing at a fast pace, whereas some remain constrained due to lack of active REITs. Countries which has established the REIT regime in this decade are in the nascent stage of the organisation. These new regimes are looking to expand their REIT knowledge to a better advantage through this investing platform.

6.4 STRUCTURES OF REIT

Real Estate Investment Trusts are tax-efficient structures for investors to invest in real estate. The regulatory framework of the system may differ from country to country. Still, all REITs' main characteristic is the revenue generation from rental collections by owning and managing the properties.

Initially established in the US in 1960, there was not much variation in REITs till the early 1990s. Later refinements in REITs structure made it an appealing vehicle for owning property. Inspired by US REITs, other countries also established their adaptations of the REIT structure. These structures can be broadly classified on a continental basis as follow:

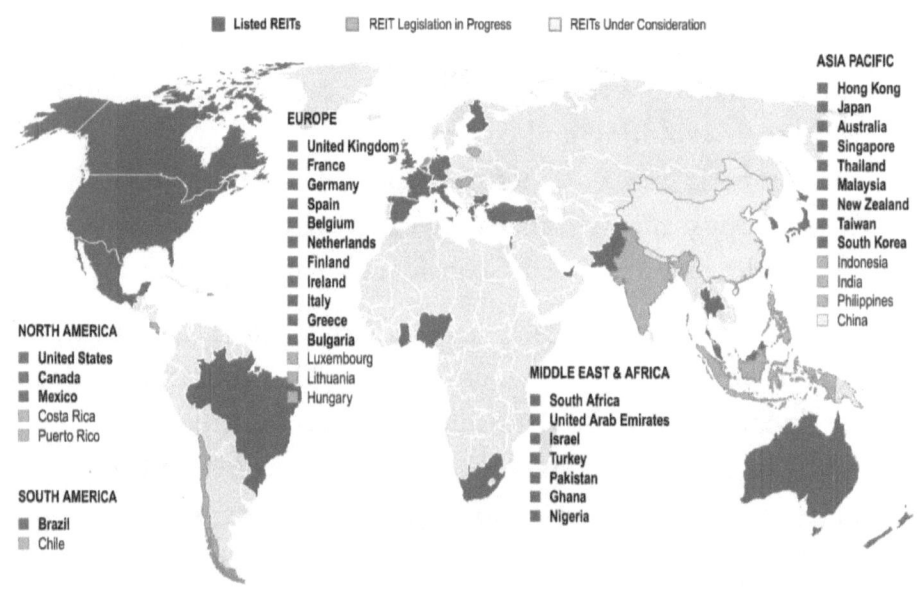

At August 31, 2017. *Source:* FactSet, Cohen & Steers

6.4.1 Americas Structure

USA was the first country to establish REIT in 1960, accounting for the total market capitalization of US $1.33 trillion as of 2019. It was created as a part of the Cigar Act; a law intended to generate wealth for individual investors. This regime paved the way for millions of investors to invest their capital into income-producing real estate. The ten largest REITs worldwide are based in the USA. Followed by which Brazil and Canada adopted REITs in the early 1900s. The regimes in Canada are the same as the US, but they pay out their dividends every month rather than a typical quarterly schedule, unlike the US. In past years, Brazil has seen significant development and increased real estate markets' investments, resulting in substantial investments into BR-REITs. The table below represents America's jurisdiction, its structure name and the number of REITS adopted.

Country	Structure Name	Year	No. of REITs
Brazil	FII	1993	159
Canada	MFT	1994	47
Chile	FI & FIP	2014	-
Costa Rica	REIF	1997	-
Mexico	FIBRAS	2004	15
Puerto Rico	REIT	1972	5
USA	US-REIT	1960	200

Source: ERPA Global Survey (2018)

6.4.2 Europe Structure

European nations are the early adopters of REITs. The Netherlands introduced its system in 1969, trailed by other countries in Central and Southern Europe. By 2013 there were a total of 14 European countries that introduced REIT regimes. In Europe, REITs were first established in the Netherlands and France, followed by the UK and Germany in 2007. According to the European Public Real Estate Association (EPRA), Europe accounts for just 21.8% of the global REITs market capitalization, estimated at €754 billion. The property market regimes within the EU are characterized by variety and fragmentation. Most of the 27 EU member states have their own funds structures and legislation. This fragmented market in the EU is than that of US or Asian markets. The current unified regimes of EU-REITs are presented below in line with the EPRA Global REIT Survey 2018.

Country	Structure Name	Year	No. of REITs
Belgium	SICAFI/BE-REIT	1995/2014	17
Bulgaria	SPIC	2004	26
Finland	FINNISH REIT	2009	1
France	SIIC	2003	29
Germany	G-REIT	2007	6
Greece	REIC	1999	5
Hungary	REIT	2011	-
Ireland	REIT	2013	4
Italy	SIIQ	2007	5
Lithuania	REIT	2008	-
Luxembourg	SIF	2007	-
Netherland	FBI	1969	5
Spain	SOCIMI	2009	59
United Kingdom	UK-REIT	2007	52

Source: ERPA Global Survey (2018)

6.4.3 Asia Pacific Structure

The Asia-Pacific REIT (AP REITs) market is the second-largest REIT market globally, representing about 32 per cent of the total global REIT-market capitalization. Inside the Asia-Pacific region, Australia and Japan are the most significant contributors. Australia is one of the largest and oldest markets, accounting for approximately 35 per cent of the area, trailed by Japan with 35 per cent, Singapore with 14 per cent, and Hong Kong with 9 per cent. The remaining 5% is contributed from other countries of Asia Pacific, such as India, New Zealand, South Korea, Thailand, Taiwan, and Malaysia. However, they constitute less than 5 per cent of the REIT market in the Asia Pacific and less than 0.5 per cent globally. Significant possibilities for growth are expected in this region if China introduces REITs into their markets.

Country	Structure Name	Year	No. of REITs
Australia	UNIT TRUST	1985	50
Hong Kong	HK-REIT	2003	9
India	REIT	2014	1
Indonesia	DIRE	2007	2
Japan	J-REIT	2000	61
Malaysia	UNIT TRUST	2005	18
New Zealand	UNIT TRUST	2007	7
Pakistan	REIT	2007	1
Philippines	REIT	2009	-
Singapore	S-REIT	1999	35
South Korea	REIC	2001	6
Taiwan	REIT	2003	5
Thailand	PFPO	1992	58

Source: ERPA Global Survey (2018)

Index Constituents - Profile

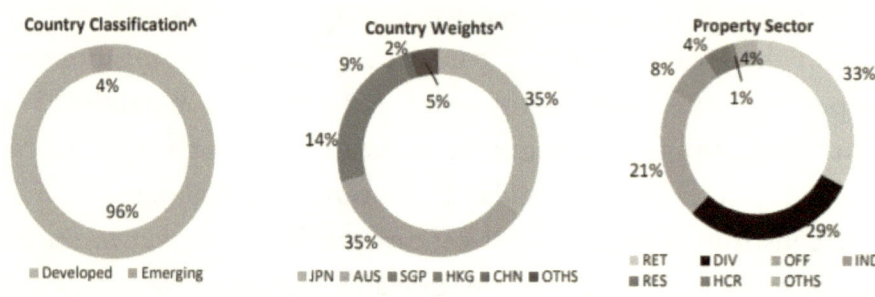

Source: GPR/APREA AsiaPac Performance Snapshot, 2017

The below table gives the snapshot of the GPR/APREA Composite REIT Country Index Year-to-December 2017 of major markets of AsiaPac. Singapore market topped the REIT total return rankings in 2017.

Also, Hong Kong REITs performed great on a 3-year, 5-year and 10-year basis. Markets of Australia, Singapore and Hong Kong shows excellent potential for an investor looking for an international approach.

% Total Returns (USD)	1yr	3yrs*	5yrs*	10yrs*
Australia	14.73	9.80	7.52	1.50
China**	24.51	·	·	·
Hong Kong	29.09	18.18	15.47	16.60
Japan	-3.56	1.49	6.34	3.97
Malaysia	21.88	5.78	2.76	9.27
Singapore	39.00	9.19	6.24	8.07
Taiwan	-0.79	-0.21	-0.39	7.39

*Annualised compound growth

Source: GPR/APREA AsiaPac Performance Snapshot, 2017

Note: **The China REIT index is an experimental addition to the series. It tracks seven REITs that hold assets located in China. At present, there are no entities listed in Mainland China.

In the Asia Pacific, the REITs are predominantly managed by REIT managers. The REIT shall pay the manager a fee in exchange for its management services. The manager features a legal duty to act within the best interests of unitholders.

6.4.4 The Middle East & Africa Structure

REITs have not yet found their root in the Middle East, with only a handful of REITs across UAE and KSA. The market capitalization of the UAE in REITS is less than 3%.

Though the REITs in the Middle East are since 2006, still it lacks a legal framework in some jurisdiction for tax treatment. If regulated properly, there is a market opportunity for REITs to grow across the Middle East. Whereas in KSA, there were sudden listings with insufficient diligence done on the quality of assets.

The number of REITs in the Middle East and Africa is as below:

Country	Structure Name	Year	No. of REITs
Dubai	REIT	2006	2
Israel	REIT	2006	6
South Africa	REIT	2013	31
Turkey	REIC	1995	25

Source: ERPA Global Survey (2018)

6.5 COMPARISON

The table summarizes the critical regulatory, operations, and establishment of REITs of the world's significant jurisdictions on a continental basis.

PARTICULARS	U.S.A	The U.K.	Singapore	India
Year Enacted	1960	2007	2002	2014
Governed by	The US Internal Revenue Code and the Treasury regulations	Tax law	Monetary Authority of Singapore (MAS) and the Singapore Exchange	Securities and Exchange Board of India (SEBI)
Formalities and procedures	1. An entity electing to be taxed as a REIT must satisfy specific organizational, asset holding, income source and distribution requirements. 2. It must elect to be taxed as a REIT or made such election in a previous taxable year.	1. Provide notice to Her Majesty's Revenue and Customs (HMRC) in writing before the beginning of the accounting period from which the regime will apply. 2. Provide various financial statement in addition to the statutory accounting statements.	1. Application to the Inland Revenue Authority of Singapore for tax transparency and tax exemption rulings	1. The REIT is to be constituted as trust and is required to be registered under the Indian Registration Act and with the SEBI to carry the activities. 2. The sponsor(s), manager and trustee should be designated, and all such persons should be separate entities.

Capital requirement	No capital requirement	No capital requirement	Minimum capital of SGD 300 million	Minimum capital of INR 5000 million
Listing requirement	No listing requirement	Mandatory listing	Listing required for tax concessions	Mandatory listing
Leverage	Not limited by legislation, but tax authorities may impose limits on the amount of related party leverage	Tax charge on REIT if the interest cover is less than 1.25:1	May exceed 35 per cent of its deposited property. Up to 60 per cent maximum if the S-REIT has obtained credit rating from either Fitch Ratings, Moody's or S&P.	The aggregate consolidated borrowings and deferred payments of the REIT net of cash and cash equivalents shall never exceed 49 per cent of the REIT assets

Minimum number of investors	At least 100 shareholders. Further, less than five individuals cannot hold > 50%	35% public float	25% of share capital to be held by a minimum of 500 subscribers	25% of public holding to be held by a minimum of 200 subscribers
Non-resident investors	Permitted to invest	Permitted to invest	Permitted to invest	Permitted to invest
Foreign assets	Investment permitted subject to conditions	Investment permitted	Investment permitted	Investment permitted
Distribution requirement	At least 90% of taxable income to be distributed	At least 90% of rental profits to be distributed	To avail tax concession, 90% of taxable income to be distributed	At least 90% of net distributable cash flow to be distributed
Timing of distribution	Annually	On or before the corporate tax filing date	Annually	Semi-annually

6.6 CORRELATIONS ACROSS BORDERS

The table below indicates the correlation between the performance of one (local or regional) real estate market that influences another real estate market's performance across borders. When investing in REITs worldwide, a low correlation of real estate markets worldwide provides the advantages of diversification and reduces volatility and risk of a portfolio.

Exhibit 6: Global Real Estate Securities 5-Year Correlations by Country

		NORTH AMERICA		EUROPE			ASIA PACIFIC		
		United States	Canada	United Kingdom	Germany	France	Australia	Japan	Hong Kong
NORTH AMERICA	United States	1.00							
	Canada	0.51	1.00						
EUROPE	United Kingdom	0.39	0.29	1.00					
	Germany	0.47	0.43	0.45	1.00				
	France	0.49	0.55	0.65	0.69	1.00			
ASIA PACIFIC	Australia	0.70	0.68	0.39	0.57	0.57	1.00		
	Japan	0.26	0.48	0.15	0.07	0.25	0.44	1.00	
	Hong Kong	0.39	0.54	0.31	0.46	0.43	0.57	0.28	1.00

At August 31, 2017. Source: Morningstar, Cohen & Steers.
Data quoted represents past performance, which is no guarantee of future results. Correlation is a statistical measure of how two data series move in relation to each other, with 1 representing perfect synchronization and 0 representing perfect randomness. Correlation analysis based on monthly data from 8/31/12 to 8/31/17. See page 7 for index associations, definitions and additional disclosures.

Source: Morningstar, Cohen and Steers (Monthly data from 31/08/12 to 31/08/17)

Note: Correlation is a statistical measure of how two data series move about each other, with 1 representing perfect synchronization and 0 representing perfect randomness.

6.7 INVESTMENT IN INTERNATIONAL REITS

International REITs currently accounts for the bulk of REITs around the world. With global success, these securities offer numerous advantages and a diversified international portfolio for an investor. For investors trying to create associate allocation to real estate can also take a globally diversified approach.

The simplest and most cost-efficient way to add a global listed real estate allocation to one's portfolio is by purchasing an investment in publicly-traded REITs, REIT mutual funds, REIT exchange-traded funds (ETFs) and closed-end funds (CEFs) that focus on these international REITs by purchasing shares through a broker. One can also buy shares of a non-traded REIT through a broker or financial advisor who participates in the non-traded REIT's offering.

The top REITs with sizeable international exposure include:

- American Tower
- Brookfield Property REIT
- Medical Properties Trust

The most popular international REIT ETFs have:

- SPDR Dow Jones Global Real Estate (RWO)
- WisdomTree International Real Estate (DRW)
- SPDR Dow Jones International Real Estate (RWX)
- iShares S&P Dev ex-US Property (WPS)
- iShares FTSE EPRA/NAREIT Dev Real Estate (IFGL)

CHAPTER 7

REITS IN INDIA

7.1 INTRODUCTION

The global perception of the Indian real estate market has changed over the years. The land acquisition act, demonetization, introduction of RERA and GST have brought about significant changes in the sector and formalized it to a large extent. With the growth in the corporate sector, the demand for commercial spaces and residential properties has increased in the past few years. It has led to an increase in the inflow of investments to the sector.

Until the past few years, banks, financial institutions and private companies have been the only finance sources for developers. As the market is growing, there is a need for modern investment options like REITs to increase funding to the sector.

Over the years, retail investors have shown a lot of interest in equity and debt instruments because of increased capital markets awareness. The government is also encouraging people to start investing in mutual fund SIPs and other investment methods. REITs give retail investors a chance to invest in income-producing real estate with small capital sizes and enhance their portfolio's diversity.

In 2008, SEBI released an initial set of regulations for REITs. Over the years, the regulations were modified under international standards by consulting various stakeholders and companies, and the final draft of the regulations was launched in 2014. A few more amendments in rules were introduced in 2016.

Timeline of REITs in India

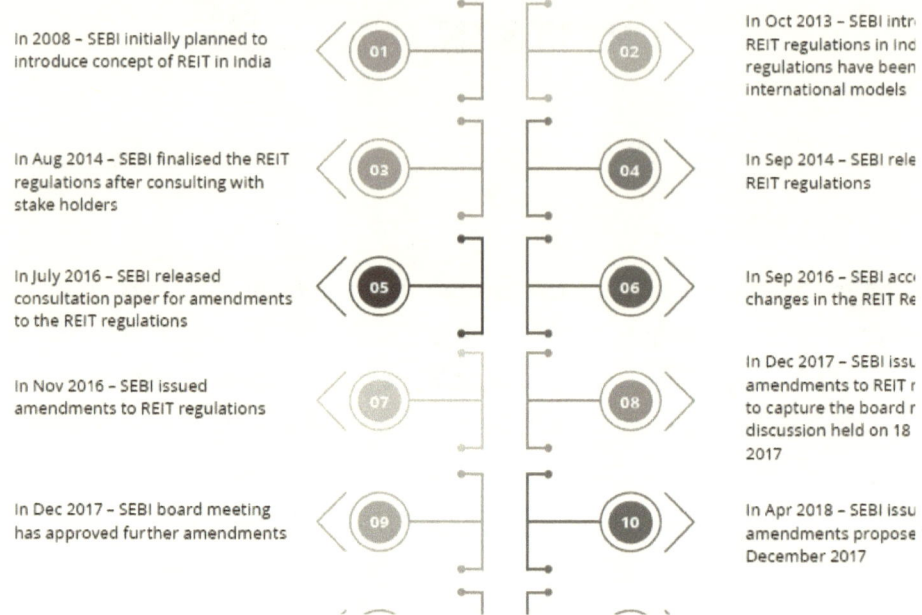

Source: Deloitte

7.2 REIT-ABLE CITIES IN INDIA

- India's financial capital, Mumbai, is considered one of India's costliest markets. The city's central business districts, South Mumbai and Bandra Kurla Complex (BKC), have a good supply of office spaces covering multiple business segments like BFSI, Consulting and Media. The peripheral business districts like Thane, Powai, Navi Mumbai have office spaces that majorly cater to the IT/ITES sector.

- Delhi, the capital city of India, has a significant share of commercial spaces in the country. The Central Business areas like K. G. Marg and Connaught place have office spaces that cater to the sectors like BFSI. Business districts like Gurgaon and Noida have offices of companies from the IT/ITES and BFSI sector.

- Bangalore is considered to be the technology capital of India. In the last two decades, it has seen significant growth in the Grade A office areas as most of the companies from the IT/ITEs sector setting up their operations in the city. One of the biggest IT companies in India, Infosys and Wipro, have their headquarters in Bangalore. The city is also known to be the favourite destination for setting up start-ups.

- Hyderabad is one of the preferred locations for companies from the IT/ITES sector. The business areas like Madhapur and Gachibowli have a significant share of office spaces in the city. Hyderabad has witnessed high rental prices and increasing demand for office spaces in the past few years.

- Chennai and Pune also have a decent supply of office spaces. The companies in these cities are mostly from the IT/ITES sector. There has been a consistent rise in rental prices in these cities.

- JLL research indicates that 294 mn sq. ft.* of office stock would be eligible for REIT. It would translate to a potential investment of USD 35 bn*. (Source)

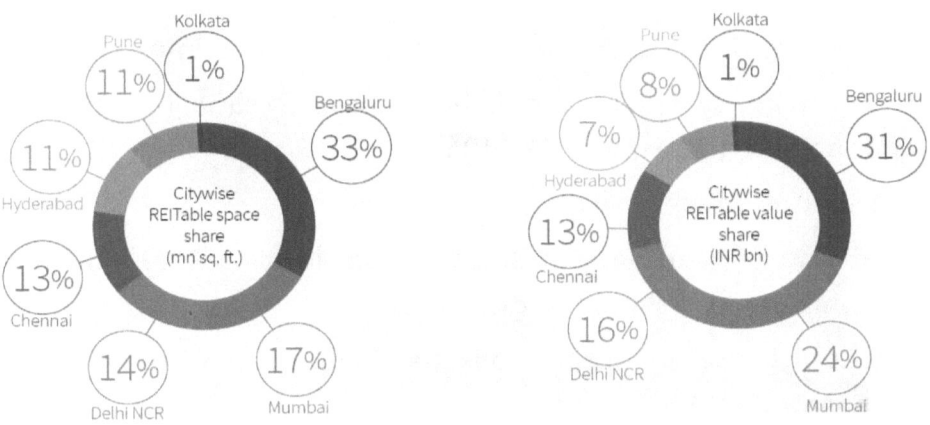

Source: JLL Report

7.3 REIT REGULATIONS

Asset-related conditions

- At least 80% of the REIT's portfolio should consist of completed and rent-generating properties. They should also have a lock-in period of at least three years from their purchase date.
- Up to 20% of the REIT's portfolio can consist of:
  - Under construction properties
  - The debt of real estate companies
  - MBS (Mortgage Backed Securities)
  - Equity in companies that generate a minimum of 75% of their income from activities related to real estate
  - Government securities
  - Unutilized FSI and TDR in the related investments
  - Money market instruments

Additional conditions

- The REITs are not allowed to invest in vacant land or agricultural land.
- Investing or lending to other REITs is also not permitted
- The stake in properties should be held directly either by the REIT or holding company or the SPV.

Distribution Policy

- At least 90% of net distributable cash flows of REIT/Holding Company/SPV should be distributed
- The disbursal of distributions should be done once every six months
- If the property sale proceeds are not reinvested within one year, then a minimum of 90% of the proceeds should be distributed to the unitholders.

Public offer

- The minimum value of assets in the REIT's portfolio should be INR 500 crore.
- The minimum size of the public float is 25%.
- The minimum offer size should be INR 500 crore
- The minimum subscription per applicant is INR 50,000
- The minimum no. of investors is 200.

Sponsors' holdings

- The sponsor should hold a minimum of 25% of the units after the IPO for at least three years. The number of units exceeding the 25% limit should be held for at least one year.
- At all given times, the sponsors should hold at least 15% of the units, and each sponsor should have at least 5% of the units.
- The sponsors can sell their units to other sponsors if they satisfy all the holding conditions and have held the units for at least three years post listing.

7.4 REIT TAX IMPLICATIONS

Taxation at REIT level

Dividend received from SPVs	Dividend income is exempted but WHT is applicable
Interest income from SPVs	Interest income is exempted
Capital gains	LTCG – 20% STCG – 30%
Other types of income	Taxable at 30%

Taxation for unit holder

Dividend received from SPVs	Dividend income is exempted
Interest income from SPVs	Resident - At the applicable tax rates
Capital gains	LTCG – 10% STCG – 15%
Other types of income	At the applicable tax rates

LTCG – Long Term Capital Gain

STCG – Short Term Capital Gain

WHT – With Holding Tax

CHAPTER 8

CASE STUDY ON REITS

8.1 EMBASSY OFFICE PARKS REIT

Embassy Office Parks REIT is India's first publicly traded REIT launched by the real estate developer Embassy Group and investment firm Blackstone. It was incorporated in March 2017 at Bengaluru, Karnataka, under the Indian Trusts Act, 1882. It was registered with SEBI as a real estate investment trust having registration number IN/REIT/17-18/0001.

Structure of the REIT

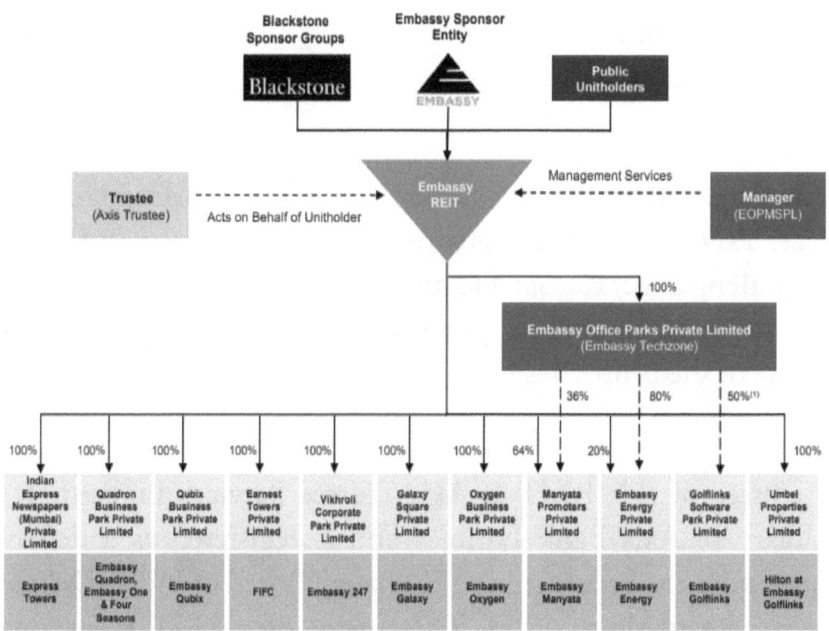

Source: Embassy Office Parks REIT – Investor Factsheet

Sponsors

Embassy Office Parks REIT has two sponsors, namely Embassy Property Developments Private Limited (Part of Embassy group) and BRE/ Mauritius Investments (Part of Blackstone Group).

The Embassy Group is one of the biggest real estate developers in India. Over the years, they have developed more than 45 million sq. ft of area and properties in hospitality and industrial segments. They have more than two decades of experience in various fields like land acquisition, design, interior designing, development, marketing and sales of properties, facilities management and corporate leasing.

Blackstone Group Inc. is an investment firm based out of the USA. It is one of the largest alternate investment companies which invests in various asset classes like real estate, private equity, public debt and secondary funds. As of 2019, the company manages assets worth $571 billion.

In June 2020, Blackstone group sold an 8.7% stake in the REIT for $300 million (Rs.2,270 crore).

Manager

The manager of this REIT is Embassy Office Parks Management Services Private Limited. It is a private limited company formed in 2014 in Bengaluru, Karnataka, under the Companies Act, 1956. The company has experience in providing property management services for some of the properties of the Embassy group.

Trustee

The trustee of this REIT is Axis Trustee Services Limited. It is a subsidiary of Axis Bank Limited and is registered as a debenture trustee under the Securities and Exchange Board of India (Debenture Trustees) Regulations, 1993. The trustee of a REIT is responsible for ensuring compliance with statutory requirements, maintaining ethical standards and best corporate governance practices.

Initial Public Offering

18 Mar, 2019	Opening Date
20 Mar, 2019	Closing Date
27 Mar, 2019	Finalisation of Basis of Allotment
28 Mar, 2019	Initiation of refunds
29 Mar, 2019	Transfer of shares to demat account
01 Apr, 2019	Listing Date

- **No. of units before issue:** 613,332,143
- **No. of units after issue:** 771,665,343
- **Total no. of units for the issue:** 158,333,200
  - Portion of Strategic Investors: 29,208,800
- **No. of units (after strategic Investor):** 129,124,400
  - Portion of institutional investor: 96,843,200
  - Portion of non-institutional investor: 32,281,200
  - **Total issue Value:** Rs. 47,499.96 million
  - **IPO Price Band**: Rs. 299 – Rs. 300
  - **Issue price:** Rs. 300

Unitholding pattern

S. No	Category of Unit Holder	No. of Shares	% of Shares
1	**Sponsors and other related parties**		
1.1	Indian	115,484,802	14.97
1.2	Foreign	359,649,988	46.61
2	**Public Holding**		
2.1	Institution	213,666,600	27.69
2.2	Non-Institution	82,863,953	10.74
	Total (1) + (2)	771,665,343	100.00

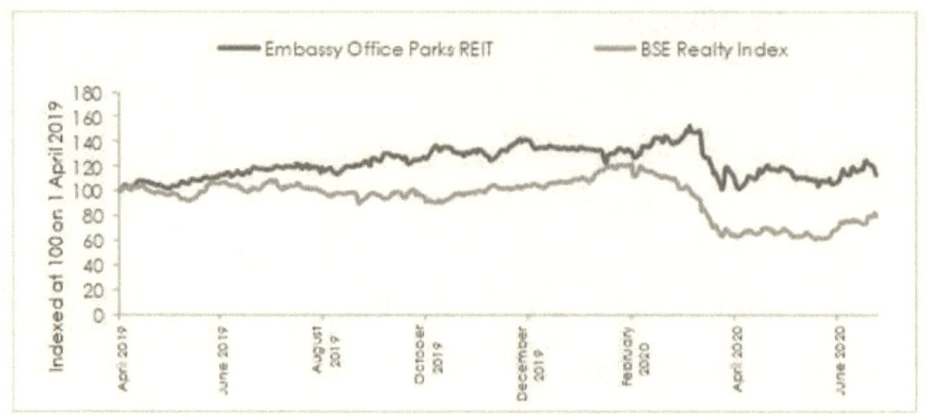

Source: www.financialexpress.com

Portfolio Information

Portfolio area	33.3 msf
Completed area	26.2 msf
Development area	7.1 msf
Hotels	1,096 keys (477 operational)
Solar	100MW
Occupancy	92.2%
Occupiers	160+

Portfolio cities

City Name	Gross Asset Value
Bengaluru	63%
Mumbai	15%
Pune	13%
NCR	9%

Office parks

Name	Area	Status
Embassy Manyata, Bengaluru	14.8 msf	Partially Completed
Embassy Golf Links, Bengaluru	2.7 msf	Completed
Embassy Quadron, Pune	1.9 msf	Completed
Embassy TechZone, Pune	5.5 msf	Partially Completed
Embassy Qubix, Pune	1.5 msf	Completed
Embassy Oxygen, Noida	3.3 msf	Partially Completed
Embassy Galaxy	1.4 msf	Completed

City centre offices

Name	Area	Status
Express Towers, Mumbai	0.5 msf	Completed
FIFC, Mumbai	0.4 msf	Completed
Embassy 247, Mumbai	1.2 msf	Completed
Embassy One, Bengaluru	0.3 msf	Completed

Hotels

Name	Capacity	Status
Hilton at Embassy GolfLinks	247 keys	Operational
Four Seasons at Embassy One	230 keys	Operational
Hilton and Hilton Garden Inn at Embassy Manyata (5-Star)	619 keys	Under-Development
Hilton and Hilton Garden Inn at Embassy Manyata (3-Star)		Under-Development

Solar parks

Name	Capacity	Status
Embassy Energy	100 MW	Operational

*msf – million square feet

Occupier Information

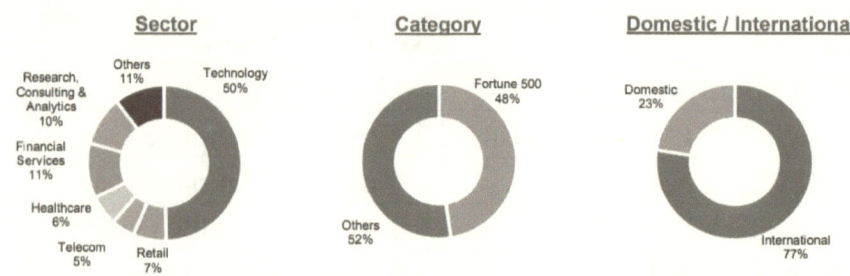

The top 10 occupiers as of June 2020 are IBM, Cognizant, NTT Data, ANSR, Cerner, PwC, Google India, Nokia, JP Morgan and Lowe's.

8.2 MINDSPACE BUSINESS PARKS REIT

Mindspace Business Parks REIT is the second publicly traded REIT in India. It was launched by the real estate developer K Raheja Corp Group in association with Blackstone Group. It was incorporated in November 2019 in Mumbai, Maharashtra, under the Indian Trusts Act, 1882. It was registered with SEBI in December 2019 as a real estate investment trust having registration number IN/REIT/19-20/0003.

Structure of the REIT

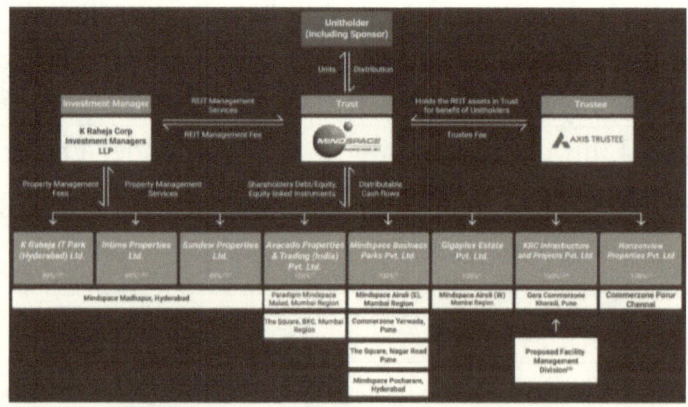

Source: www.mindspacereit.com

Sponsors

Mindspace Business Parks REIT sponsors are Anbee Constructions LLP (ACL) and Cape Trading LLP (CTL). Both the companies are registered as LLPs under the LLP Act and are a part of the K Raheja Corp Group.

K Raheja Corp Group is a real estate developer based out of Mumbai. The company has over four decades of experience in the development and operations of properties in multiple asset classes. As of 2020, the company has developed an area of 28.5 million sq. ft.

Manager

The manager of this REIT is K Raheja Corp Investment Managers LLP. It is an LLP that was formed in February 2018 with ID no. AAM-1179. The firm undertakes real estate development, offers project management services and provides all services required to manage the REIT.

Trustee

The trustee of this REIT is Axis Trustee Services Limited. It is a subsidiary of Axis Bank Limited and is registered as a debenture trustee under the Securities and Exchange Board of India (Debenture Trustees) Regulations, 1993. The trustee of a REIT is responsible for ensuring compliance with statutory requirements, maintaining ethical standards and best corporate governance practices.

Initial Public Offering

27 Jul, 2020	29 Jul, 2020	04 Aug, 2020	05 Aug, 2020	06 Aug, 2020	07 Aug, 2020
Opening Date	Closing Date	Finalisation of Basis of Allotment	Initiation of refunds	Transfer of shares to demat account	Listing Date

- **No. of units before issue:** 556,654,582
- **No. of units after issue:** 593,018,182
- **Fresh issue:** 36,363,600
- **Total no. of units for sale:** 163,636,200
  - Portion of Strategic Investors: 40,909,000
- **No. of units (after strategic Investor):** 122,727,200
  - Portion of institutional investor: 92,045,400
  - Portion of non-institutional investor: 30,681,800
- **Total issue Value:** Rs. 45,000 million
- **IPO Price Band**: Rs. 274 – Rs. 275
- **Issue price:** Rs. 275

Unitholding pattern

S. No	Category of Unit Holder	No. of Shares	% of Shares
1	**Sponsors and other related parties**		
1.1	Indian	37,48,97,081	63.22
1.2	Foreign	0	0.00
2	**Public Holding**		
2.1	Institution	17,53,13,301	29.56
2.2	Non-Institution	4,28,07,800	7.22
	Total (1) + (2)	59,30,18,182	100.00

Portfolio Information

Portfolio area	29.5 msf
Completed area	23.0 msf
Under construction area	2.8 msf
Future development area	3.6 msf
Occupancy (committed)	92.0%
Occupiers	170+

Portfolio cities

City Name	% of Gross Asset Value
Mumbai	41.1%
Hyderabad	39.3%
Pune	16.9%
Chennai	2.7%

Business parks

Name	Leasable Area
Mindspace Airoli East, Mumbai	6.8 msf
Mindspace Airoli West, Mumbai	4.5 msf
Mindspace Madhapur, Hyderabad	10.6 msf
Commerzone Yerwada, Pune	1.7 msf
Gera Commerzone Kharadi, Pune	2.6 msf

Office buildings

Name	Leasable Area
Paradigm Mindspace Malad, Mumbai	0.7 msf
The Square, BKC	0.1 msf
Mindspace Pocharam, Hyderabad	1.0 msf
The Square, Nagar Road, Pune	0.7 msf
Commerzone Porur, Chennai	0.8 msf

*msf – million square feet

Occupier Information

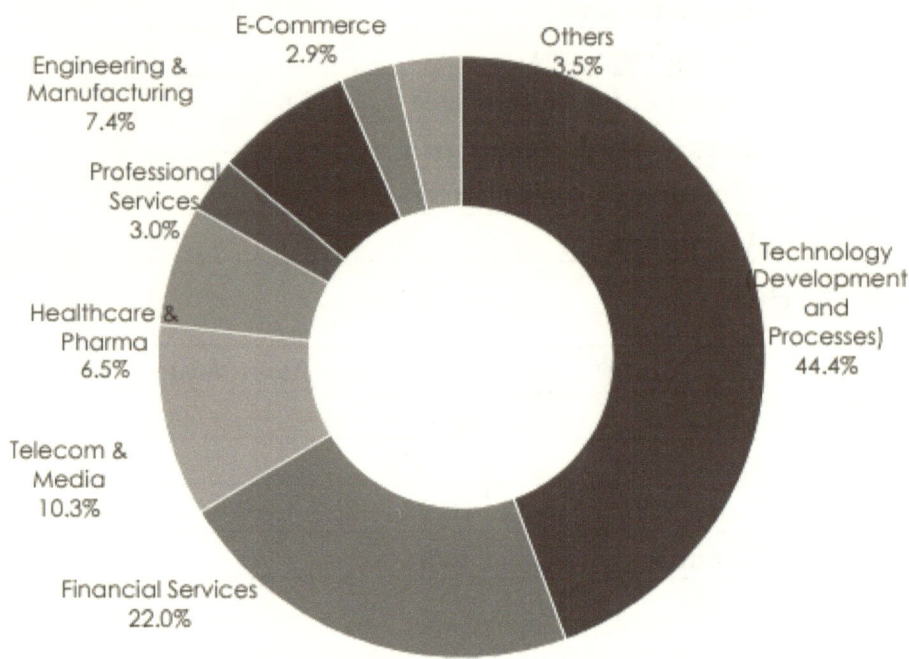

Source: Factsheet-of-Mindspace-Business-Parks-REIT

8.3 BROOKFIELD INDIA REAL ESTATE TRUST

Brookfield India Real Estate Trust is India's third and only institutionally managed public commercial real estate company. It is sponsored by an affiliate of Brookfield Asset Management (BAM), part of Brookfield Group. It was registered with SEBI as a real estate investment trust having registration number IN/REIT/20-21/0003. It was incorporated on February 17, 2021 with IPO worth Rs 3,800 crores which saw a subscription of nearly 8 times.

Structure of the REIT

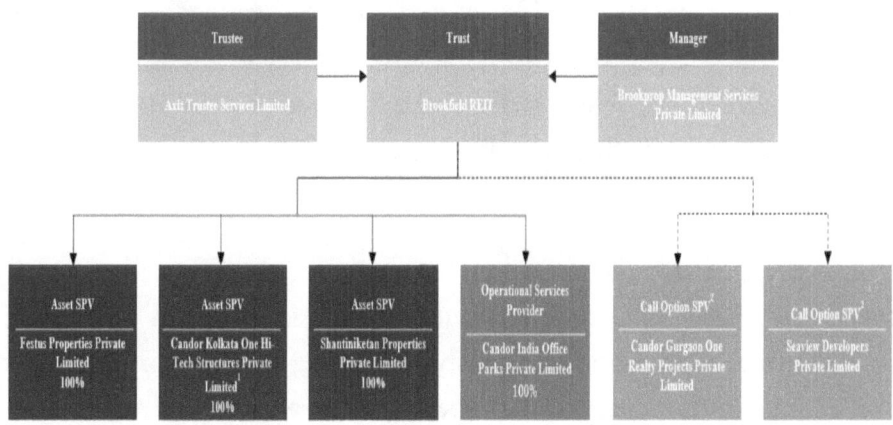

Source: Brookfield India Real Estate Trust – Draft offer document

3 Sponsors

Brookfield India Real Estate Trust is sponsored by an affiliate of Brookfield Asset Management (BAM), one of the world's largest alternative asset managers and investors. As of September 30, 2020, it has approximately US$575 billion of assets under management, across real estate, infrastructure, private equity, renewable power and credit strategies. Also, BAM has a global presence of over 150,000 operating employees across more than 30 countries.

In long term, the business will be supported by Brookfield Asset Management's extensive local market and asset knowledge in India. It has a decade-long presence in India and manages a portfolio of approximately US$17 billion across real estate (US$4.6 billion), infrastructure (US$9.7 billion), private equity (US$2.1 billion) and renewable power (US$ 0.6 billion) as of September 30, 2020.

Manager

The manager of the REIT is Brookprop Management Services Private Limited. It provides management services, including facility management and project delivery to the real estate assets held by Brookfield Group in India. It has a net worth of Rs. 141.02 million.

Trustee

The Trustee of this REIT is Axis Trustee Services Limited, a wholly-owned subsidiary of Axis Bank Limited. It is involved in varied facets of debenture and bond trusteeships, including advisory functions and management functions. Also, it acts as a security trustee and is involved in providing services of security creation, compliance and holding security on behalf of lenders.

Initial Public Offering

Issue Opening Date	03 Feb, 2021
Issue Closing Date	05 Feb, 2021
Finalisation of the Basis of Allotment	11 Feb, 2021
Transfer of shares to Demat Account	12 Feb, 2021
Listing Date	17 Feb, 2021

- **No. of units before issue:** 164,619,801
- **No. of units after issue:** 302,801,601
- **No. of units (after strategic Investor):** 138,181,800
  - Portion of institutional investor: 103,636,200
  - Portion of non-institutional investor: 34,545,600
- **Total issue Value:** Rs. 83,270 million
- **IPO Price Band:** Rs. 274 – Rs. 275
- **Issue price:** Rs. 275

Portfolio Information

Portfolio area	14.0 msf
Completed area	10.3 msf
Under construction area	0.1 msf
Future Development area	3.7 msf
Committed Occupancy	87 %
Occupiers	117

Portfolio cities

City Name	% of Gross Asset Value
Mumbai	22.2%
Gurugram	38.2%
Noida	17.3%
Kolkata	22.3%

Office buildings

Initial portfolio (14.0 msf)

Name	Leasable Area
Kensington, Mumbai	1.5 msf
Candor Techspace G2, Gurugram	4.0 msf
Candor Techspace N1, Noida	2.8 msf
Candor Techspace K1, Kolkata	5.7 msf
CIOP	-

Identified Assets (8.3 msf)

Name
Candoe Techspace G1, Gurugram
Candor Techspace N2, Noida

ROFO Properties (6.7 msf)

Name
Powai Business District, Mumbai
Equinox Business Park, BKC
Units in Godrej, BKC
Waterstones, Mumbai

Occupier Information

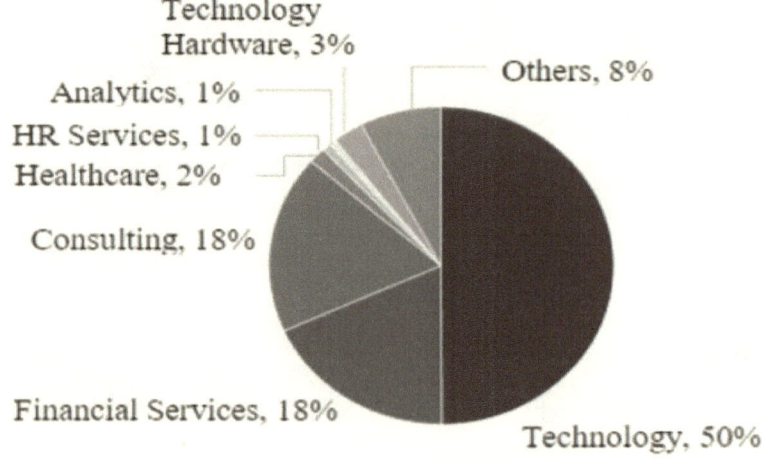

Source: Brookfield REIT Final Offer Draft

CHAPTER 9

FRACTIONAL OWNERSHIP

Fractional ownership is an investment method where multiple parties, individuals or companies who are mostly unrelated, jointly own an asset of high value. The main reasons for opting for fractional ownership are mitigating the risk among the several entities and sharing the maintenance costs.

Fractional ownership is mostly done in the case of tangible assets like:

- Aircrafts
- High-end cars
- Yachts
- Real estate properties

Usually, an asset's management is done by an organization that maintains and operates the property on behalf of the owners. The company also collects the revenue generated (typically from renting it out) from the property. It distributes it to the owners as per their percentage of ownership after deducting management fees and expenses.

9.1 FRACTIONAL OWNERSHIP IN REAL ESTATE

For a very long time, investment in real estate has been thought of as a way people with monetary advantages could only access it. However, with the emergence of new technologies and increasing awareness about the market, the thought is changing fast.

Fractional real estate investment is a method where multiple people come together to buy shares of a property. This property ownership type can be implemented in assets like hotels, resorts, residential buildings, vacation homes, resorts and other commercial establishments.

9.2 HOW DOES FRACTIONAL OWNERSHIP WORK?

Source: assetmonk

- Initially, a company, which is in the property management business, identifies properties that have the potential to return a high yield. Those properties are acquired at the best price possible.

- Each of these properties is broken down into smaller units (also referred to as fractions) based on their total value. The total value of each asset includes all the additional costs like taxes, legal fees etc.

- These units are listed on the company's portal, which investors can purchase.

- After purchasing units, a shareholder's agreement is to be signed by the investors who have all the details about rules and regulation, capital contributions, maintenance, ownership rights, usage of the property, investment amount and fraction of ownership.

- After the sale deed is registered, each co-owner is provided with a fractional ownership certificate.

- According to their share of ownership, the revenue (rental income) generated, or the expenses incurred from the property, would be borne by all the co-owners.
- The company also collects a management fee for maintaining the property.

9.3 STRUCTURE OF FRACTIONAL REAL ESTATE OWNERSHIP

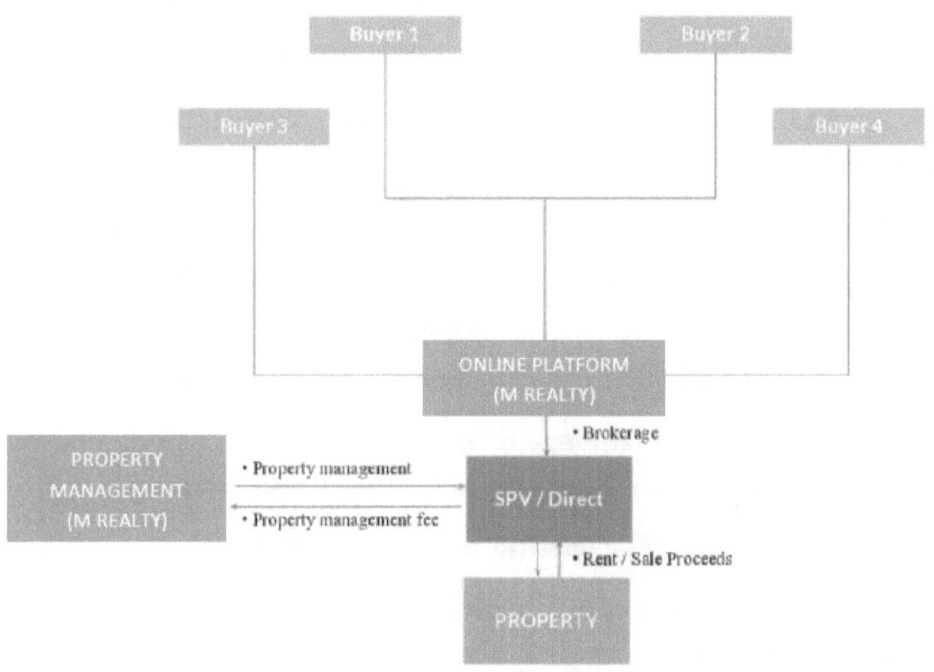

Source: M Realty

9.4 TYPES OF FRACTIONAL REAL ESTATE OWNERSHIP

- **Commercial usage**

    This type of fractional ownership can be seen in commercial spaces like hotels, office spaces and warehouses. As owners do not frequently use these types of properties, they are leased out to other companies. The rental income received is distributed to all co-owners based on the percentage of their share. The asset management company which manages the property is paid a portion of the revenue as a fee.

- **Personal usage**

  In this fractional ownership model, all the co-owners get their share in the usage of the property. This model is implemented in properties like vacation homes, resorts and residential complexes. During each owner's share of time in the year, the property is either kept for personal use or rented out to others.

9.5 VALUATION OF FRACTIONAL OWNERSHIP INTEREST

Valuators generally uses two valuation approaches and methods to value a real estate fractional ownership property, namely:

1. The Income Approach and the partition analysis valuation method which is used to value an income fetching property
2. The Market Approach and the sale transaction analysis method which is used to value non-income fetching property

Income Approach – The Partition Analysis Method

It is an income approach valuation method. The method involves valuing a fractional interest in real property with a discount factor being applied to that fractional interest.

The steps involved in valuing a partial interest are:

1. Identify the Market Value of the subject property
2. Calculate the proportionate share value in the property on a pro-rata basis by taking the 100% value of the property times the percentage of property owned
3. Less the pro-rata proportion of real estate partition cost

4. Determine an appropriate discount for the partial interest
5. Calculate the value of the fractional part by multiplying the value of the proportionate share times the discount rate

The real estate partition cost generally includes:

- the expense of the partition lawsuit
- the time required to complete the lawsuit
- the structural and engineering cost to divide subject property physically
- the uncertainty related to a real estate partition action

The several factors that influence the discount rate are:

- the number of owners
- the proportionate share
- the use of land
- the cost of real estate partition
- the availability of finance

Market Approach – The Sale Transaction Analysis Method

This approach involves comparing fractional interest to published studies of empirical data of nearby fractional interest sales. The steps involved in valuing property includes:

1. Identify the Market Value of the subject property
2. Review the physical and economic characteristics of the subject property and its relevant real estate market
3. Then the value is adjusted for any outstanding mortgages or other encumbrances. It is termed as adjusted net asset value (Adjusted NAV)

4. Compare the subject property ANAV with published studies of empirical data on actual sale transactions and determine an appropriate discount factor

5. Calculate the value of the fractional interest by multiplying ANAV times the discount rate

The discount factor derived from actual market transactions gives combined price adjustments related to:

- Discount for lack of control (DLOC) is the amount or percentage decreased from the value of an ownership interest to reflect the relative absence of some or all of the powers of control.

- A discount for lack of marketability (DLOM) – a percentage decreased from the value of an ownership interest to reflect the relative absence of marketability.

9.6 ADVANTAGES OF FRACTIONAL OWNERSHIP IN REAL ESTATE

1. It allows the buyers to own a luxurious vacation property in exotic locations at an affordable price. Also, the investors have to pay only a part of the operating costs of the property. All the expenses related to renovation, furnishing, housekeeping and taxes will be split among all the co-owners.

2. By opting for the fractional ownership method, investors can buy stakes in multiple properties instead of investing in a single property.

3. Investing in income-generating properties gives a substantial rental income to the buyers.

4. The management of the property can be handed over to asset management companies. They look after the regular upkeep of

the property and ensure the monthly collection of rentals. The owners can be free of any worries about maintaining the property.

9.7 FRACTIONAL OWNERSHIP VS TIMESHARE

	Fractional Ownership	Timeshare
Equity Ownership	The user's share value varies according to the market conditions	Buyers only get usage rights and not ownership
Title Deed	A title deed is registered for all the co-owners	The holding company holds the title deed
Management	Owners control management of the property	Users have no say in the management of the property
Maintenance expenses	Owners should pay their share of taxes and expenses	Users should pay the monthly charges and expenses
Resale	As the value appreciates, it is easy to sell ownership rights	It is difficult to resell timeshares as the value doesn't appreciate easily

CHAPTER 10

GLOBAL FRACTIONAL OWNERSHIP

10.1 FRACTIONAL OWNERSHIP IN THE USA

The fractional ownership industry was first started in the US. It was first implemented in the Rocky Mountains ski resorts in the early 1990s. These first fractional developments realized that people didn't want to buy entire houses, which they would use just for a few weeks a year in the mountains. So they came up with fractional ownership of property wherein the people can share the houses.

Fractional property gives investors real estate ownership while at the same time providing more leisure time and a second home in the desired location. In recent years, fractional ownership has offered an alternative to timeshares and full ownership of a vacation property. The U.S market provides a range of opportunities to consumers. Currently, there are 126 Active Fractional Properties around the United States, including equity funds that invest in vacation homes.

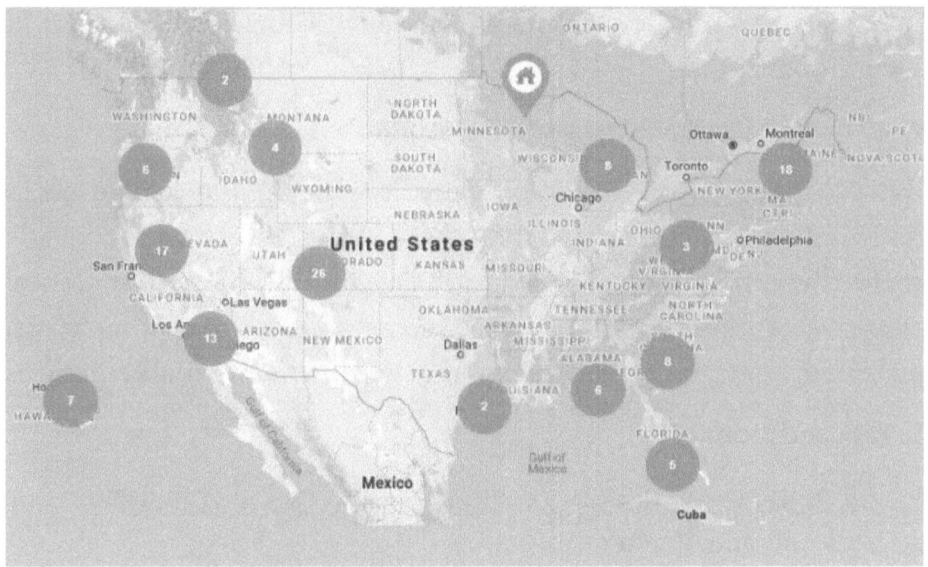

Active U.S. Fractional Properties

U.S. Fractional Ownership Properties and Usage Options

With more than 50% of fractional ownership properties offering 4-6 weeks per year, this is the most popular usage option available across the U.S. market. Second, it is 10-12 weeks per year.

10.2 FRACTIONAL OWNERSHIP IN SINGAPORE

In Singapore, FO is offered over second homes, resorts as well as commercial assets. With blockchain technology's utilisation to tokenize investment in real estate, the Singapore-based investment platform Shareable Asset (SA) enables investors to fractionally own institutional-grade real estate assets. Of the five financial technology-driven securities companies utilising blockchain technology that has been approved in the city-state. Previously, it was almost impossible to own a part in these types of real estate investments. These assets, which could be corporate properties in prime locations in major cities worldwide, have only been made available to institutional or high net-worth investors. But with the adoption of fractional ownership in Singapore with the tech based-firm allowed investors to invest in such properties.

Overview of Shareable Asset (Case Study):

By redefining conventional investments with the blockchain-based tokenisation structure, Sharable Asset allows investors to quickly create diversified portfolios and capitalize on the ability to trade real estate assets online and in real-time securely. Ownership of fractional real estate assets has provided investors with attractive market returns

Legal conditions:

- All properties and money shall be held in trust in each user's name with the designated custodian.

- A seamless digital know-your-customer (KYC) process integrated with the Singapore Government-powered MyInfo service enables new users to register for their Shareable Asset account with pre-filled personal data from MyInfo.

- There should be compliance with Anti-Money Laundering (AML) regulations.

- All financial transactions and the ownerships of assets are reported in a transparent, immutable distributed ledger leveraging blockchain-convergent technology.

- Consumer safety is provided with industry best-practices, including two-factor authentication, data encryption during transit and authentication of the communication network with Transport Layer Security (TLS) protocol.

- The highest degree of cybersecurity with improved infrastructure, resilience practices that include vulnerability evaluation and penetration testing, access controls, information security, data protection, network security and patch management.

Benefits

Singapore based company offers a new way for asset owners to sell their assets. It provides opportunities for smaller investments, verifying real estate properties, non-physical, simple investor onboarding, hassle-free digital purchase of global real estate once an account has been created with the firm.

It allows investors a simple-to-use interface that will enable them to conveniently pick from the list of equity and debt investment products with the app's help, with a minimum investment of one-hundred Singapore Dollars (SGD 100) per asset. Asset owners may now be encouraged to sell a portion of their properties or raise debt on their properties with a hassle-free experience and limited paperwork and benefit from the extensive listing of assets made available to investors worldwide.

Security Token

 24/7 markets

 Fractional ownership

 Rapid settlement

 Increased liquidity & market depth

 Flexibility of smart contracts

 Automated compliance

 Reduction in direct costs

 Asset interoperability

Shareable Asset's tech-forward platform dramatically decreases the time spent on transactions and paperwork for real estate stakeholders, including those brokers as well as developers. It helps the stakeholders concentrate on value-added factors that optimise their projects' success and deliver good returns.

10.3 FRACTIONAL OWNERSHIP IN AUSTRALIA

Fractional property investment in Australia is relatively a new concept in the market, and currently, there are a limited number of start-ups that offers such a platform in Australia. The two leading fractional investment platforms in Australia are BRICKX and DomaCom.

BRICKX uses a buyer agent and property market analysts to identify the properties with good rental returns and scope of capital appreciation. Then they buy these properties and split the total investment into 10,000 shares, or "Bricks". Now the investors can purchase and sell these Bricks on the platform and receive monthly rent payments based on their investment size.

DomaCom pools the funds from investors to purchase properties. The platform allows users to contribute funds along with other like-minded investors toward an asset for sale. Once the required number of investors have contributed, the property is purchased and is operated as a Managed Investment Scheme (MIS). DomaCom also provides a platform that enables investors to sell their shares to other investors.

Here's an example of its layout:

The third fractional investment site CoVESTA has recently joined the Australian market. CoVESTA operates in the same way as BrickX and DomaCom. Still, it also has the added advantage of enabling investors to identify and live in their property if they prefer to. All they need to do is find a property they want to live in and start the "Invest & Rent" syndicate, and once the alliance is closed, they become the tenant of the property.

Returns in Australian markets:

In the first place, income returns can be minimal. Most investors rely on market capital growth, which means that if the market picks up by 10%, a unit or brick will also increase by around 10%.

Investors might like better to actively trade their bricks, buying and selling regularly within the hopes of picking a quick profit. However, with transaction costs being added to most transactions, this might be a quick way to erode capital. Each property's ongoing expenses (insurance, council, fees, maintenance, etc.) are paid for out of the tenant's rental income for all the platforms. Much like the method of selecting a managed fund, the success of a fractional investing opportunity comes right down to the fees to be paid and, therefore, the investment potential and returns from the property chosen.

10.4 FRACTIONAL OWNERSHIP IN LONDON

Fractional ownership in London is a good investment opportunity for frequent travellers and also ordinary people. The Fractional ownership properties in London are usually managed by the owners of the resort in which they are located. Depending on terms and conditions, the purchasers may informally or on a commercial basis, let their friends share their shares. And hence, due to their share of the property, they share its financial fate whether it appreciates or depreciates.

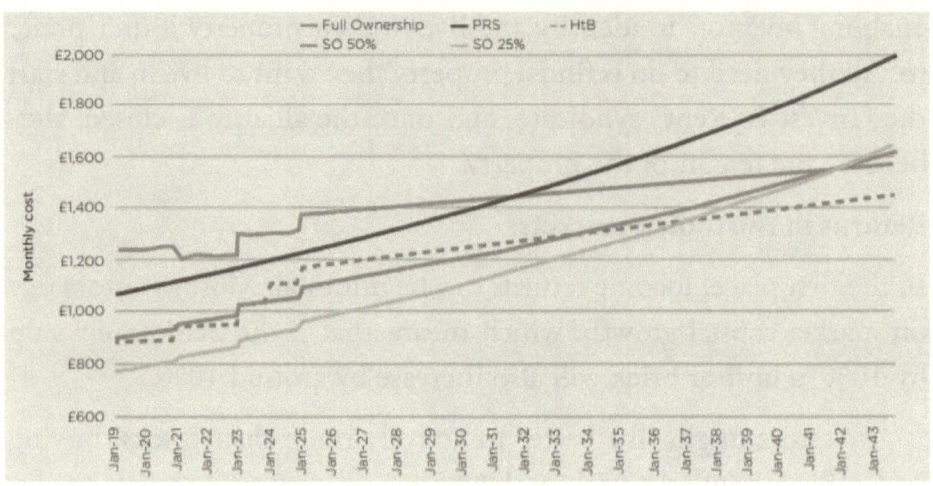

Source: Savills Research using Oxford Economics, Bank of England | **Assumptions**

Market overview

Some players in London are offering one-10th shares in the property. This ownership allows the purchasers the exclusive use of the properties for five weeks per year. There are smaller homes available for most other fractional ownership projects, whose units can be bought in one-10th, one-15th or one-20th shares.

Problems faced in FO (London)

Investors of legitimate and good-quality FO homes may find it challenging to secure a mortgage if they cannot afford to buy a share in cash. It's not feasible to get a mortgage as multiple buyers of one property mean that lenders can't take security on it. The fact that all of these schemes are overseas makes lenders even more hesitant.

10.5 SUMMARY

Every country observes a different pattern or system of fractional ownership globally. Some countries are new to this concept, while countries like the USA thrive on this system in their holiday regions.

Second homes, resorts, and commercial properties are part of real estate that categorizes under fractional ownership in most parts of the world.

Most countries are adapting the online platform listing method for Fractional Ownership. As it has provided a better alternative for a timeshare, it holds immense potential for growth globally, considering its risks and returns.

CHAPTER 11

INDIAN FRACTIONAL OWNERSHIP

11.1 INTRODUCTION

The idea of fractional ownership in real estate has been predominant in the US and Europe for a decade and is presently on India's rise. It is in nascent stages in India, with a modest bunch of real estate online platform offering this service. These are mainly tech-based start-ups that have utilized the technology to build a forum where investors could come together to own a property fractionally. Some tech-based start-ups that have ventured into Indian markets include Strata, PropertyShare, FRACSN, hBits, RealX, etc. In India, fractional ownership is now a $5 billion market and is rising daily.

Fractional ownership provides flexibility in the portfolio of the investor. Commercial real estate (CRE), such as office spaces, warehouses, and retail, has been highly leveraged because they are the best performing asset classes in rental yields and capital appreciation. As a result, a broad investment portfolio has been offered in this category. The residential asset class is seen as an opportunity to purchase a fully furnished and professionally managed second home for use, rent and sell after, in the long run, sell after appreciation.

11.2 PROPERTIES

Any asset which generates rental yield and can be split into fractions can be brought under fractional ownership. Typically, fractional ownership properties are large multi-unit projects developed and sold by prominent real estate players to firms with the requisite knowledge in investment and property management who leveraged and monetized these assets. These investments can be carried out from large commercial spaces to even second homes assets. Profits can be generated from a curated portfolio of commercial, co-working, co-living, high-end retail, hospitality, warehousing, and residential asset classes by investment across India's fastest growing location. The ticket size of investment starts from as low as 10 Lakhs to 25 Lakhs based on its investment criteria. It enables an investor for small-ticket investment in high-grade properties.

Currently, Fractional Ownership in India being in its initial stages; the portfolio of assets offered for the investment are:

1. Commercial Office Spaces

    Investment in A-grade commercial properties (CRE) with small ticket size across Tier 1 and Tier 2 cities of India such as Mumbai, Bengaluru, NCR – Delhi, Hyderabad, Chennai, Pune has now become possible with fractional ownership. A good rental yield of 7 – 10% and long-term capital appreciation can be gained through investment in these properties.

2. Warehouses

    With a shift in global supply chains from China to India, a significant penetration of e-commerce and manufacturing industries will boost India's warehousing facilities in the coming years. Warehouses are rapidly rising as a potential investment, and leveraging it with fractional ownership will promise good returns to the investors.

3. Residential

    US and European markets have extensively exploited the residential markets. They have seen second homes, vacation homes and resorts as an excellent opportunity to monetize them. A very few firms in India that have entered residential asset such as second homes and studio apartments since the returns on investments in these assets are low compared to that of commercial.

4. Land

   A large area of land is generally plotted and split into fractions. Also, an option of ready to built land with a project plan is being explored under fractional ownership.

11.3 OWNERSHIP STRUCTURE

For every property, a Special Purpose Vehicle (SPV) is created. The SPV can either be registered as a Limited Liability Partnership (LLP) or a private limited company. All the investors are either partners/shareholders in the SPV.

Once the property is fully funded, the investors will transfer that amount into the SPV, which will purchase the property on behalf of the investors. In most cases, the sale deed will have the names of all the investors.

A co-ownership agreement is recorded between the investors who set out costs involved, the owners' rights and responsibilities. The decisions regarding the property manager's appointment, tenant allocation, and other issues are taken through a voting process.

The ownership details are maintained in government records, public databases and the FO Company's platform. In India, the ownership data is recorded with the Ministry of Corporate Affairs and Blockchain platforms (if the company uses Blockchain technology).

11.4 FINANCING THE INVESTMENT

Investors can choose to finance these types of investments through personal equity or debt. As of November 2020, Indian banks do not give home/property loans to invest in fractionally owned properties. The investors might have to opt for a personal loan for investing in such properties.

11.5 REGULATORY AUTHORITY

As of November 2020, there is no set of fixed regulations for fractional ownership of India's real estate properties. Most of the companies that facilitate fractional ownership of real estate assets are registered with SEBI. Some of the companies have registered for testing under the regulatory sandbox.

In June 2020, SEBI released the framework for the regulatory sandbox. Under section 12 of the SEBI Act, 1992, the companies have to be registered to be allowed for testing under the framework.

The regulatory sandbox is a testing environment that allows companies to experiment with new Fintech (financial technology) solutions in a live and controlled environment on a limited number of customers for a specific period. It helps companies to use innovative solutions and promotes the growth of financial markets. After the testing phase is completed, SEBI decides whether to allow the FinTech solution to be introduced into the market.

11.6 TAXATION PROCESS

The SPVs get their returns in rental income (from leasing the property) and capital appreciation (upon the property sale). The rental income is taxed in the hands of the SPV and is distributed to the investors in the form of dividends.

Some of the investments are structure in the form of Compulsory Convertible Debentures (CCDs). In that case, the interest income received by the investors is taxed according to their income tax slabs rate.

For investors who are residents in India, in most cases, a 10% TDS is deducted before distributing the income.

At the time of exit, if the property is sold at a higher price than the price at which it was purchased, a capital gains tax has to be paid by the owners. As of November 2020, the tax slabs for capital gains from a property sale are as follows:

Tax type	Applicable tax
Short Term Capital Gains tax (held for less than two years)	According to the Income-tax slab rate
Long Term Capital Gains tax (held for more than two years)	20% (with indexation benefit) & 10% (without indexation benefit)

Source: myloancare. in

11.7 DUE DILIGENCE PROCESS

Firms have a dedicated team of experts who carry out thorough due diligence before investing in any property. It involves technical, financial and legal due diligence. Due diligence is mandatory and essential to mitigate any risk of investment and assure good returns from the asset. Series of steps are followed before finalizing the property for fractional ownership.

1. Stringent selection criteria

   Screening of properties is carried out based on the industry-specific criteria is met for a good location, building grade and specifications, rental yields and appreciation, market demand, tenant profile and sale price.

2. Technical and legal due diligence

   The screened properties are then checked for technical and legal due diligence from competent counsellors to avoid any legal obligations on the asset. A law firm carries out verifications of all the government permits and clearances for the building from various departments. It ensures that the building completely compliant with all the local and central government regulations without any violations.

3. Financial due diligence

   Financial cash flow models are run on the property to forecast the property's growth in yield and capital appreciation and meet the investment gaps. A detailed study is carried for rentals, expenses such as asset maintenance, property tax payments, Common Area Maintenance (CAM) charges, etc., to formulate the expected IRR for the investments.

4. Listing

   After screening and due diligence, the properties generating better returns and appreciation are shortlisted and are listed on the firm's portal for an investment opportunity.

11.8 FEES CHARGED

The fractional ownership firms charge a property management fee which may vary from property to property and firm to firm. Usually, the fees charged to the investor ranges from 0.5% - 1%. This property management fee shall cover asset management costs, the expenditure of maintenance, rent collection, GST payouts, TDS payouts, property tax, compliance of the SPV, dashboard portal, and distribution charges to the investor. The management fee is recovered from the gross rentals at the time of monthly distribution to the investors. Any additional fee may be charged if any customer requests physical financial & due diligence reports or track records of the asset. Investors will not be charged for any management fees if the tenants do not lease the property.

In some instances, if any property appreciates higher than the returns promised on capital appreciation, a performance fee of 10 – 20% on capital appreciation above the guaranteed return will be charged at the time of sale of the asset.

The firm maintains the contingency reserve from investors to cover any unforeseen expenses in the asset if they occurred. If these funds are unused, they will be refunded to the investor at the property's sale time.

11.9 DOCUMENTATION

Investors:

The investors need to undergo specific documentation to get registered with the firm and purchase the property. The documentation process will depend based on the firm you choose to invest through. Some of the documents required during the transaction of the property are as follow:

- Identification Proof
- Address Proof
- PAN Card
- A cancelled cheque
- 16 digit Demat account number
- Relevant SPV agreement/Ownership Agreement
- Property Management Agreement

The following documents can be signed either physically or digitally. Many regimes have implemented digital signatures to make the process faster and transparent for their customers.

Fractional Ownership Firm:

Investors are provided with certain documents as evidence of their transaction and ownership of the property. And all the details of ownership, the relevant reports and the track record can also be accessed by the customer via a dashboard on the firm's platform. The investors are provided with the following documents:

- SPV Agreement/Ownership Agreement
- Sale Agreement
- Lease/Rental Agreement
- Title report
- Tenancy details
- Due diligence reports

The ownership of the property through SPV is documented with the Registrar Of Companies (ROC) under the Ministry of Corporate Affairs at relevant state offices. And the regime, such as Fracsn and RealX, has deployed Blockchain technology to record the transaction, rendering them highly secure. It helps preserve the information in government records, public databases, and the firm's dashboard, which provides the investor with a sigh of protection against his investment.

11.10 EXIT POLICIES

Every property has an initial lock-in period post which an investor is allowed to sell his property. This lock-in period may vary from 6 months to 2 years, depending on the fractional firm through which you invest in the property. Before selling, a property should have an investment lifespan of 3-5 years, allowing the asset to appreciate. However, an early exit is possible, but this may impact the total return on the investment. Any investor who wishes to exit the investment can adopt one of these two initiative offered by the regime:

Property Sale

Once a property has reached a certain maturity period of 3 to 5 years, the customers are permitted to sell the property basis on the voting majority of the shareholders. If at least 75% of shareholders vote to sell, the firm will liquidate the property. Once the investment has been sold, the sale proceeds will be credited to the investor's registered bank account after deduction in fees and taxes. However, if the shareholders vote to hold the property, the property owner will be retained with the investor's inflow of rental yields. And the process will be surpassed to the next annual voting poll of the shareholders.

1. **Private Sale**

   An investor is free to sell his fraction to any of their subjects who comply with the guidelines. The investor must notify the firm of the sale to support and facilitate the transfer of shares and update their records. An investor can choose between the NAV (Net Asset Value) offered by the firm or at any price he wishes to sell to his subject.

2. **Resale Market**

   Every firm has a listing of resale properties on its dashboard. As a result, an investor wishing to sell the property could list their fractional property on these resale market. After the new buyer purchases, these properties, the sale proceedings' gains are credited to the investor's registered account.

11.11 RISKS

The investments in fractional real estate are speculative and may entail a substantial risk of loss. The performance and the valuation of any property are subject to general economic conditions and threats to the property market, impacting potential income distributions and capital gains/losses.

Any fractional regime gives no guarantee on returns. While rental yields are known in advance on most of the properties listed on the website, there is always a chance that the yield will not be payable as assured due to underlying real estate asset and leasing risk.

There are various risks associated, such as:

1. **Leasing Risk or Tenant default**

   Commercial leases of an investment property can significantly influence the property's value. The tenant who adheres to the lease terms is also a risk beyond the Manager's control. Disruption or expiry of the existing lease resulting in vacancy could diminish investors' actual return as the Trust's income will decrease, and the property's value may be affected.

2. **Market risk**

   Investment returns are affected by general market conditions and may decline over short or extended periods due to market sentiment, economic, technological, legal, social and political factors. Such factors are beyond the influence of the firm.

3. **Interest rate fluctuations**

   Interest rates may rise or fall over the investment duration, affecting the property's income and resale value and, therefore, the value of the firm's investment in the property.

4. **Regulatory changes**

   The ownership model is not being regulated yet. The introduction of any new legislation by SEBI may have an impact on the investment.

5. **Projected returns**

   The Information Memorandum contains projections based on many factors beyond the Trustee's control, such as rental rates for the property, interest rates and other costs associated with the property. Forecasts in this IM are not guarantees of future performance and involve known and unknown risks. Investors should be aware that actual results can differ from projections.

6. **Unexpected capital expenditure and the destruction of a building**

   Capital works may be required on the property, which may not have been budgeted. In these circumstances, the Trustee may need to use cash reserves or additional borrowings or reduce distributions to meet the extra expenditure.

7. **Liquidity risk**

   If an investor wishes to sell his property, the firm cannot convert an asset into cash without giving capital and income due to a lack of buyers.

Each firm has a dedicated team of experts who carry out proper market analysis with external due diligence before leasing any property to mitigate these risks to ensure healthy returns for its investors. However, before any investment decision is made in real estate, it is suggested that the financing should be consulted. And always read through the property documents to understand the risks in detail provided by the regimes.

11.12 INDIAN FRACTIONAL REGIMES

India is in the nascent stage of the development of Fractional properties. So far, a few tech-based companies have come up with this model to support the investment and heal the ailing Indian real estate sector. Some of the namely fractional ownership startup in India are (Data as of Feb 2021):

Company	Strata
Website	strataprop.com
Location	Bengaluru, Chennai, Mumbai, Hyderabad
Min. investemnt	Rs. 25 Lacs
Propeties offered	Warehouses (4) and Office spaces (3)
Properties	Strata Avigna I, Strata Avigna II Brigade Metropolis, Eagle Burgman, etc

Company	Propshare Capital
Website	Propertyshare.in
Location	Bengaluru, Pune, Mumbai, Hyderabad
Min. investemnt	Rs. 9.75, 10, 24 & 25 Lacs
Properties offered	Office Spaces (19)
Properties	Brigade Tech Park, The Pavilion III Mindspace Business Park, IBC Knowledge Park, etc

Company	FRACSN
Website	Fracsn.in
Location	Siruseri, Sholinganallur
Min. investment	Rs. 4, 5 & 10 Lakhs
Properties offered	Studio Apt., Office Space (1), Land
Properties	Studio Apt, Prestige Cyber Tower

Company	hBits
Website	Hbits.co
Location	Mumbai
Min. investment	Rs. 10 & 25 Lacs
Properties offered	Office Spaces (4)
Properties	Ackruti Centre Point, 41 Der Deutsche 42 Der Deutsche Park, 32 Der Deutsche Parkz

Company	AcreShare
Website	Shareacre.com
Properties offered	Residential real estate

Company	BRIK itt
Website	Brikitt.com
Location	Goa
Properties offered	Residential real estate, Resorts

Company	Renivesh
Website	Renevish.com
Location	Delhi-NCR, Noida
Min. investment	Rs. 25 Lacs
Properties offered	Office Spaces (3)

Company	RealX
Website	Realx.in
Location	Ahmedabad, Gurugram, Pune, Bhiwandi
Min. Investment	Rs. 5 & 50 Lacs
Properties offered	Hotel (1), Office Space (1), Residential (1), Industrial Asset (1)
Properties	Milestone Experion Centre, Nisarga Vishwa

CHAPTER 12

BLOCKCHAIN IN REITS AND FO

12.1 WHAT IS BLOCKCHAIN?

Blockchain is a digital ledger which is used to record all the transaction of an asset. It works on the principle of an open distributed ledger system that all the computers in the network can manage. All the system transactions are recorded in the form of blocks connected in the form of a chain. Each block has a timestamp and is highly encrypted, making it difficult for the users to tamper with the transactions. It creates high transparency in the system and builds trust.

In the beginning, the blockchain was used to implement digital currency like bitcoin. But in recent years, few technology companies have been using the asset tokenization method to develop transparent ownership system for various assets.

What is asset tokenization?

Asset tokenization is the process of dividing an asset into multiple tokens based on its value. Like an initial public offering (IPO) in share markets, these tokens are released on online portals, which investors can purchase. A single token usually represents a percentage of shares in the asset.

Asset tokenization is implemented using blockchain technology through which all the transactions regarding the asset are recorded into the ledger. Blockchain technology also helps in implementing smart contracts, which makes the trading process hassle-free for investors.

Property tokenization is the process of converting the value of a real estate asset into digital tokens. These digital tokens can be purchased by investors, which gives them a partial ownership right to the property. Unlike traditional real estate investments, which involve lock-in periods, these units can be traded at the investors' comfort and need. It makes real estate accessible to a wide range of investors.

As property tokenization is done using blockchain technology, some of the fraudulent activities like tampering of the transaction, selling of units to multiple people and falsification of documents can be prevented up to a large extent. Also, all the middlemen who are usually involved in a real estate transaction are eliminated, which reduces the costs, decreasing the risk and increasing liquidity.

12.2 BLOCKCHAIN IN REIT

Real estate transactions may sometimes be incredibly complicated, time-consuming, and expensive. Developers, real estate agents, banks, local people, the government needs to check and sign off their transactions before it can get done. This complexity and regulations require middleman at every point, and we have to pay more significant cuts to them. That's where Blockchain comes into the picture. This technology can make the process of buyers and sellers in Real Estate much easier.

If we codify local and national housing regulations on the blockchain, smart contracts could drastically simplify the process. A prospective seller can send location, desired price and some other ownership information to the agreement. Then, pulling from a database of rules and regulations around the resale of real estate in sellers' location, the smart contract could generate contract deeds, tax records, and anything required to make the sale of the house instantly.

The purchaser can then meet the seller, negotiate on pricing terms, and then send their digital signature to the contract verifying their purchase and updating all the documents. It requires back-end work with provable and verifiable identities on the blockchain to ensure that there can be no disputes regarding signing. Similarly, the land will need to be safely and explicitly registered on the blockchain to ensure easy ownership transfer.

To make a technological advancement in the Real Estate sector and to make the transactions more reliable and cost-effective Global REIT is an initiative that came up with the adaptation of Blockchain technology in its REIT module.

Global REIT

Global REIT is the first-ever Blockchain-based REIT to be launched in the worldwide world. It has applied blockchain technology to the real-world REIT model. Unlike traditional REITs, it makes use of blockchain to pay out dividends to its subscribers.

The Sharia-compliant Global REIT acquired assets in UAE initially and will spread its root worldwide. The first Asset under Management (AUM) had a Net Asset Value (NAV) of USD 75 million. The total portfolio value of Global REIT is estimated to scale up to USD 10 billion by the end of 5 years.

Methodology

The initial coin offering (ICO) is structured so that each investor will be issued two tokens. The ICO offers the dual utility tokens to its subscribers in a respective 25-75 split:

- Global REIT Fund Manager Token (GREM)
- Global REIT Asset Token (GRET)

Global REIT Fund Manager
(GREM)

The dividend on GREM Token will initially start at 2% of NAV and will reduce to maximum of 1.25% of NAV as the Global REIT matures

Global REIT Asset Token
(GRET)

The dividend on GRET Token will be at the stable 8% of the investment made in AUM

Source: Global REIT

Technology

To introduce blockchain in the regime, the Global REIT has built a robust platform on the Ethereum blockchain, leveraging smart contracts' strength to create custom asset tokens (GRET). Along with it, the platform also enables secondary tokens GREM. This token allows investors to engage directly in dividends from the Global REIT Fund Manager. Since both the token are ERC20 standard, they are fully tradable on all token exchange platforms. This model has provided multiple investors with a more straightforward, rapid and risk-free solution to revolutionize real estate investments.

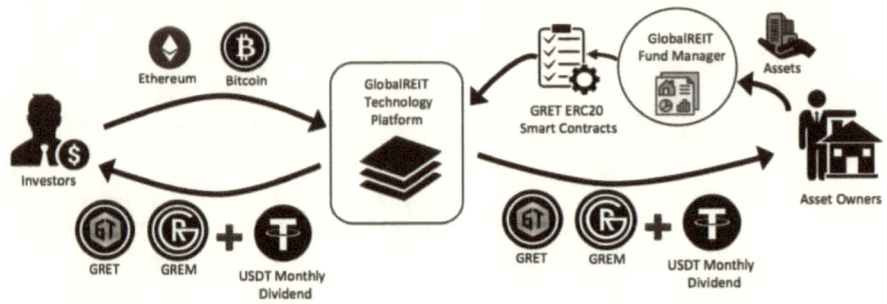

Source: Global REIT

Platform

The Global REIT platform for its core functions is a set of the following modules:

1. **The Asset Management Module**

    This module takes care of both the front end and the back end of all assets listed on the platform. End users get to see asset listings, values, historical information, market trends and a wide variety of additional information on each asset listed, which the asset management module passes to the transaction module. The backend function of the brilliant contract execution associated with the GRET token is also handled. The module is the backbone of the platform.

2. **The Transaction Module**

    It handles all API and interface calls with the external world and validates all transactions with the Asset Management Module and the Compliance Module. The module executes all central business logic for the platform, and it is responsible for the execution of instructions from all participants in the ecosystem.

3. **The Compliance and Security Module**

   The Compliance and Security Module provides a 24/7 security platform for safe transactions to investors and owners by implementing thorough industry-standard checks and balances on transacting parties, ensuring fraud elimination across the system. The system integrates military-grade security measures and protocols in addition to third-party integrations with top KYC and AML vendors to ensure system reliability, uptime, and threat prevention.

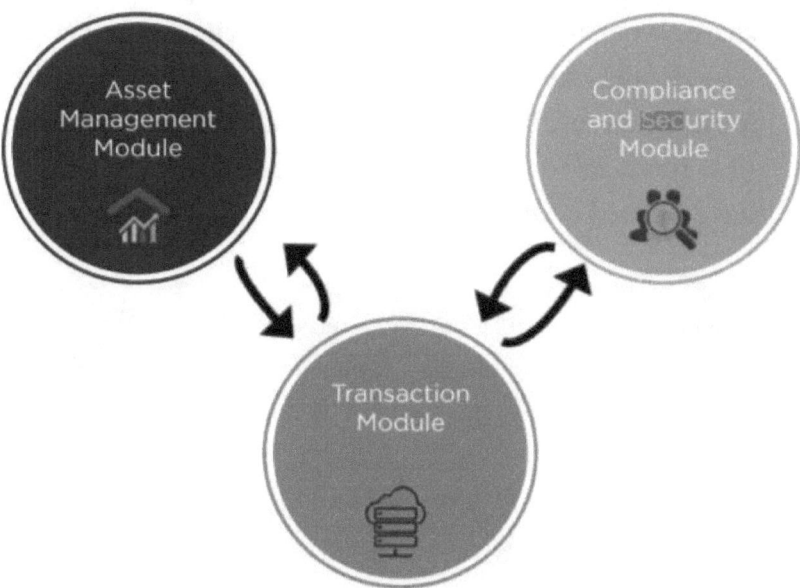

Source: Global REIT

Global REIT provides additional benefits for its token holders, which are not offered by traditional REITs, such as:

- Stable and instantaneous monthly dividends
- 'Fund Management Income' participation
- The asset portfolio of Global REIT acquired globally

- Future access to all its Assets under Management (AUM) with discounts and free stays every year in its hospitality asset
- Reward points in the loyalty program attached with the AUM

12.3 BLOCKCHAIN IN FRACTIONAL OWNERSHIP

The four critical components involved in the building of fractional ownership on the blockchain are:

- **Property listing and tokenization**

    Developers and individual owners looking to raise funds or share ownership of their property list their asset on the portals. The details like address, information about owners, images, location are available to all users. Some of the information, like financial details, ownership documents, market data, have limited access.

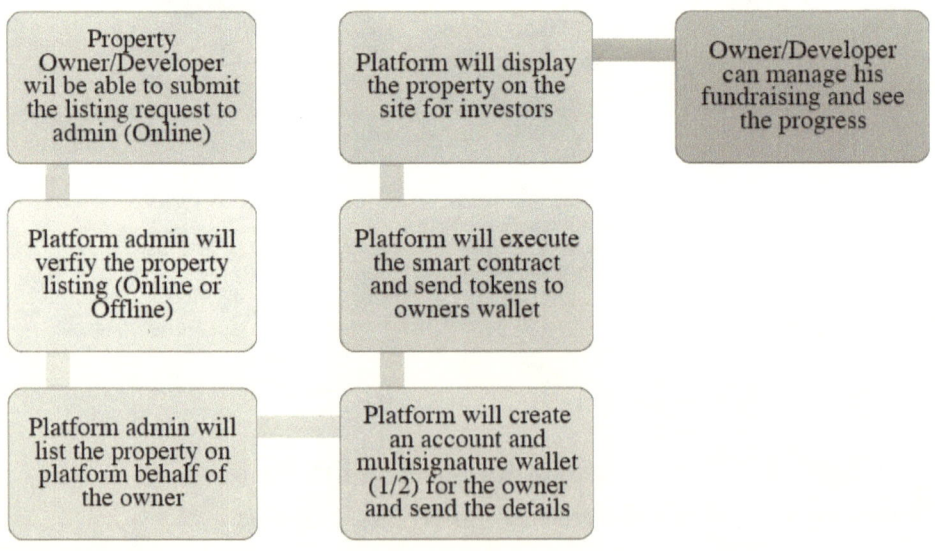

Source: medium.com

- **Property investment**

    This stage involves the identification and verification of genuine investors. In most companies, this process involves KYC and AML verification through extensive documentation and background check. After the users are verified, they can start investing in properties. They can either use the primary wallet method or direct bank transfer to an escrow account for payments.

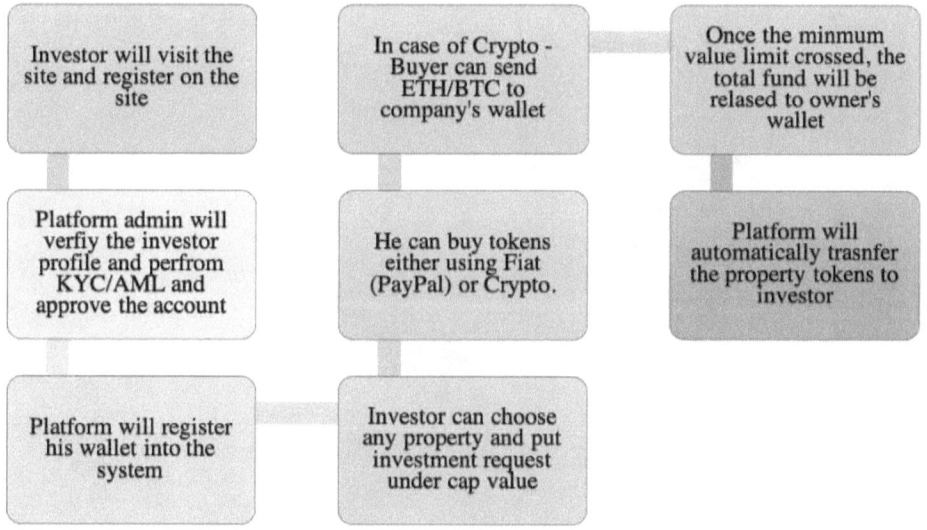

Source: medium.com

- **Profit distribution system**

    One of the most common ways of generating revenue from real estate assets is through rental income. The process of rent collection is taken care of by a property management company. A detailed ledger is maintained for each property where all the transactions are displayed. Through blockchain, the profit distribution system is automated. The amount is distributed on time as per the shareholding pattern of every user.

- **Investment liquidation**

    Investment liquidation is one of the most critical processes in the system. It should be conducted according to the legal framework of the company. The platforms can either use an inter-property exchange model or a secondary model for liquidating the investments.

www.ingramcontent.com/pod-product-compliance
Lightning Source LLC
Chambersburg PA
CBHW030759180526
45163CB00003B/1088